# Imperfectly natural
## baby and toddler

### How to be a green parent in today's busy world

# Janey Lee Grace

Copyright © Janey Lee Grace 2007

The right of Janey Lee Grace to be identified as the author of this work
has been asserted by her in accordance with the
Copyright, Designs and Patents Act 1988.

First published in Great Britain in 2007 by
Orion Books
an imprint of the Orion Publishing Group Ltd
Orion House, 5 Upper St Martin's Lane,
London WC2H 9EA

1 3 5 7 9 10 8 6 4 2

A CIP catalogue record for this book is available
from the British Library.

ISBN-13: 978 0 75286 947 6

Printed in Spain by Cayfosa-Quebecor

The Orion Publishing Group's policy is to use papers that are natural, renewable and recyclable and made from wood
grown in sustainable forests. The logging and manufacturing processes are expected to conform to the environmental
regulations of the country of origin.

Every effort has been made to fulfil requirements with regard to reproducing copyright material. The author and publisher
will be glad to rectify any omissions at the earliest opportunity.

Whilst every effort has been made to ensure the accuracy of information contained in this book, the reader should be
reminded that the book contains the author's personal views. Neither the author or publisher can take responsibility for the
effectiveness of any product or service recommended, nor can they accept any responsibility for any reader's reliance on any
information provided in this book.

www.orionbooks.co.uk

To everyone embarking on their 'imperfectly natural' journey.

Remember: 'All these ripples of holistic living will one day

add up to a sea of health.'

# Contents

# Looking After Yourself 152

# Family Lifestyles 194

# Introduction

If the closest you've ever come to natural parenting is buying your baby the reduced-sugar variety of baked beans, this book is for you. If your first child screamed and kicked through the first two years of its life, rejected the cot and the buggy and refused to take a bottle and you want the next time to be different – this book is definitely for you.

Welcome to **Imperfectly Natural Baby and Toddler**, a collection of tried and tested tips for parents who would like to live as holistically as they can while bringing up babies and young children. 'Imperfectly' is the really important bit of this title. You want to be a wonderful mother, you want to live naturally and you want your children to be healthy and happy, but you're only human. The reality is that there are times when the kids are cranky, the telly's blaring out, you're shouting like a fishwife and you're about to resort to junk food and E numbers. Don't worry, none of us gets everything right and most of us find that when we become parents we seem to inherit a new middle name – 'guilty'. Plus, today's new parents have the environment to worry about too!

I will be pointing you in the direction of holistic but realistic living – babies and children don't come with a manual and it's a steep learning curve! This book is for all parents who want to do the most natural things they can – albeit imperfectly. If you knew where to find the best nappy rash cream without any

chemicals – you'd buy it, right? If you could get advice on what to do for certain ailments without resorting to medication – you'd take it, right? The tips in this book will fast-track you to the best treatments, products and ideas to support and enhance your parenting experience. Everything that is recommended has been tried and tested by me throughout my four pregnancies or by one of my colleagues or friends who have shared their own inspirational parenting tips.

Let's not forget you! This book is **Imperfectly Natural Baby and Toddler** but it's not just about the children – we need pampering too! The Imperfectly Natural parent has to remain sane in all of this, so see the chapter Looking After Yourself (page 153), which is dedicated to helping you stay happy, fulfilled and healthy during this precious time.

As in my first book, **Imperfectly Natural Woman**, I won't go into too much in-depth technical information or analysis of the products or treatments I recommend. I figure that, like me, you're busy and will settle for whether or not something works

and forego the scientific knowledge. Wherever possible, however, I'll provide references and web addresses so that you can do more research if you want to.

I hope you'll find this book useful and inspiring. If you take up even just a few of these ideas, you'll be living more simply, often saving money and doing your bit to raise the next generation of happy, secure children who take responsibility for their environment and their health.

I hope you'll try some of the ideas in this book and I hope you'll share some of your ideas with me.

There is a thriving forum at **www.imperfectlynatural.co.uk** with a section on natural parenting – come on in and tell us what you agree with and what you don't.

# From newborn to toddler

'A baby is God's opinion that the world should go on.'
CARL SANDBURG

Congratulations! You're home and in one piece – well, two pieces as you've probably got a baby attached. Welcome to the glorious world of parenting. I remember getting back from the hospital with my first baby, just three days old, lying him down in his Moses basket and wondering what to do next. I didn't have to wonder for long. The baby let me know in no uncertain terms that he was having none of that 'lying down on his own' business. I quickly picked him up, breastfed again (wasn't it only ten minutes since he'd had a feed?), and life went on like that for the next couple of years, give or take popping out to work and having another baby.

Babies are 'all consuming' in the best possible way. Every single thing you do from now on will need to be prefaced with a thought concerning your baby's welfare. Does he need more food? If we go out now will he sleep in the car and then not sleep tonight? Is it normal to cry for that long? Don't panic, you'll handle it beautifully. You're a mum (or dad) and if you trust your intuition, that's all you'll need to get you through – with a bit of help from well-meaning like-minded mums like me. The only thing that gives me the right to share some of this with you is that I've been there four times. I've been through the steep learning curve of never intending to have any children and, somehow, joyously ending up with three boys and one girl; all healthy, all gorgeous. I'd love to guide you through some of the highs and lows you'll meet along the way, not with loads of technical jargon but with lashings

of imperfectly natural tips and ideas. Why use synthetic chemicals when there are great natural alternatives? Why not reduce your impact on the planet if it's quick, easier and healthier for you and your baby? It's a rollercoaster but it's a laugh a minute.

## Babymoon

Why 'babymoon'? Because those first few weeks when you bond with your baby and just delight in this amazing new phase of your life should be just like a honeymoon. The expression 'babymoon' has been rather hijacked in the United States by expectant couples wanting time alone before their baby is born. For me, it describes beautifully that period of calm after the birth when you celebrate the arrival of your newborn child.

Ideally, you should be able to put your feet up, breastfeed on demand and be pampered. Other cultures are fantastic at this. In India, it's common for mothers to rest for forty days in their mother's home, enjoying daily massages to restore muscle tone after the birth. Nutritious food is brought to them by attentive family members and neighbours. Sadly, across most of the Western world, we're lucky if we get a couple of days lolling around and, even then, we'll be making our own meals.

Try to get the rest you need and deserve. If your partner has paternity leave, together you can make this adjustment to family life an easier process. It will need a bit of pre-birth planning. Think ahead about how the 'domestics' of the house can survive for a few days without you, then you can hole up in your own space with your baby, settle into a rhythm and establish feeding without worrying too much about what's going on elsewhere. Place a 'Do Not Disturb' sign on the door and admit only those visitors bearing gifts of food.

There's a fair bit of adjusting to do both physically and mentally. As a mum, you're getting used to motherhood, your partner is getting adjusted to fatherhood and your baby is getting used to life outside. Don't feel pressurised into getting back to normal faster than everyone else. Revel in it all for a while and get waited on by everyone. You'll remember these first few precious days forever.

You will never have a time like this again. Even if you have another baby, there'll be a sibling or more around, so the dynamic will be different each time. Enjoy the very brief quiet before the storm. This is the start of a lifelong love affair.

# Recovery after birth

I can't beat about the bush on this one. I don't think anyone prepared me for how knackered I would feel after giving birth. If you've had a relatively good natural birth

with the minimum of intervention then at least you'll get back to normal quicker than if you've had a Caesarean. If you've had an epidural or forceps were used, it will also take its toll.

My first labour was extremely long and I did not sleep or eat for about thirty hours. After the baby was born, I put him to the breast immediately and my body literally shook with a mixture of exhaustion, euphoria, exhilaration and extreme hunger! About an hour later, while he was weighed and checked, I was checked over and then had toast and butter and the best cup of tea I'd ever tasted. Once back in bed and while my husband held his new heir, everyone was telling me to try to get some rest. I vaguely remember wanting an extra pillow but asking for something incomprehensible. I was delirious with tiredness.

## Going to the loo

Once I'd had some sleep, I remember needing to go the loo and being absolutely terrified that the pain would be worse than the actual birth. Nothing prepares you for the soreness, particularly if you've had stitches. The best tip is to get a jug of tepid water and pour it over your vagina as you urinate for the first few times. This helps to soothe the whole area by diluting the acidity of the pee. Don't expect to open your bowels for a few days; it's normal to be a bit constipated after delivery. Just drink

lots of water to ease the process. When you do manage to go, don't panic, it will feel as though your nether regions will drop away too, but they won't. If you've had stitches, you can hold a pad against the area. Your midwife will advise you on this.

## Breasts

They'll most likely feel a bit sore initially, but when your milk comes in at around day three or four, your breasts will suddenly balloon up and probably feel very uncomfortable. The best advice is to put cabbage leaves in the fridge and then lay them over your breasts; it feels wonderfully cooling. The other thing you can do if your breasts feel really engorged is to have a warm bath, put hot flannels on them and stroke downwards towards your nipples. You can use a soft body brush in the same way to encourage the milk ducts to become unblocked – I've even used a comb.

## Skin and hair

Sadly, the glow may be over. Sometimes after giving birth you feel as though the 'blooming' phase was a long-forgotten dream. Your hair can look dull and lifeless and, what's worse, start falling out big-time. Don't worry, it's all that excess hair you grew during pregnancy. Your skin may feel dry or greasy or you may even get spots. If you are breastfeeding, your little cherub will be depleting your essential minerals in huge doses so make sure you eat well. You may also have stretch marks and extra moles or brownish red marks. Basically, it's all down to your body readjusting. You'll also need to recognise you're feeling stressed, tired and emotional. Soothing baths with a good dose of Himalayan salt added will help the healing process and smothering yourself in gorgeous scented coconut oil will make you feel so much better (see Looking After Yourself, page 153).

## Bleeding

I hadn't realised quite how much you bleed after giving birth and that this can continue for up to six weeks. If you find you're bleeding excessively, get it checked out and if there are huge clots of blood or placental tissue appearing, call your doctor or health visitor. It's probably just a natural clear-out but on these issues, even natural old me says call in the cavalry!

You'll find that the blood looks very red to start with but will soon turn brownish and then almost pink. Obviously, because of the risk of infection, you can't wear tampons or even use a mooncup (see page 159) at this stage as it would make you feel even more sore, so you will need thick maternity pads. Cloth pads are perfect if you can keep up with the washing. If you're buying disposables, get the organic night-time maternity pads from Natracare (**www.natracare.co.uk**). The homeopathic remedy Caulophyllum can also help to reduce lochia (discharge), but always get advice first.

## Perineum

If your perineum was torn or cut and you have had stitches, you may well be reading this while sitting on a rubber ring! Fortunately, you do not now have to borrow your nephew's rubber ring with a bright blue duck design as The National Childbirth Trust (**www.nct.org.uk**) makes a specially designed inflatable cushion called a 'valley ring'. You can also get gel-filled pads, which can be cooled and are very soothing, but I'd suggest getting a compress of cold water soaked in calendula oil, which is healing.

## Pain

I don't think anyone prepares you for after-birth pains. It seems mightily unfair that, having had 'Braxton Hicks' contractions for four weeks, then an inordinate amount of pain during labour, you should then have to contend with what feels like period pains for a couple of weeks after the birth. You will find that the more you breastfeed, the worse the pains will be but the good news is, all the time the baby is suckling in the first few days, it's helping to send your uterus back down to where it needs to be, taking your wobbly post-birth tummy with it (hopefully!). Don't be surprised, by the way, if you still look pregnant after giving birth as that's another one of life's unfair tricks but, trust me, it will reduce in time. If it doesn't, well who cares? You may be imperfect but you're carrying a gorgeous baby to cover up all the bulges.

Take arnica tablets, preferably 200c, which will help with the shock, the bruising and the healing process generally. Chamomilla 30c is also good for pain and, if you've had a Caesarean, Calendula 30c will also help with the healing, as will Staphysagria (see Natural Medicine Cabinet, page 139).

Don't even think about trying to do pelvic floor exercises until about week six. It's then advisable to try to incorporate them into your daily routine as you did when you were pregnant. If you don't do them, you might regret it later whenever you laugh or sneeze! You should also do the post-natal exercises that are given to you by the midwife or health visitor.

## Backache

You may have backache, particularly if you had an epidural, and in my case I had very sore arms from hanging on so tightly during the pushing stage to my poor Darling Husband (DH). He also had bruised forearms from my grip and we never heard the end of that! After my fourth baby I got awful tingling pains in my legs too and panicked that I might have a deep vein thrombosis. It turns out

it was just the strain of squatting during the labour and the extra weight I was carrying.

The Bowen Technique (**www.thebowen technique.com**), a very unintrusive gentle manipulation massage, can work wonders if the aches and pains persist. Also, if you can find a therapist, there's nothing more relaxing than creative healing, another very gentle form of massage. To find a practitioner, go to **www.gentlebirth method.com**.

If possible, have a massage daily for a few days after the birth. If you don't want to use a therapist, ask your partner to massage your neck and shoulders, back and legs gently. Use a few drops of essential oil in carrier oil. Rose otto is very uplifting and Lavender is healing and relaxing.

## Your emotions

After that initial euphoria, be prepared for your hormones still playing their own game of musical chairs. You may have thought you were grumpy or irrational during pregnancy, but that will probably seem entirely reasonable compared to how you are likely to feel after the birth.

You may also find your memory and concentration seriously lacking. I found myself unable to remember where the children's socks were kept in my house;

not funny when you've got two little boys to dress and a sock monster! (Is it just me or does a monster who eats one of each pair of socks live in your house too?) Don't fall about laughing, guys. I know it's a favourite gag that women can't reverse into parking spaces, but it's not something I ever had a problem with until after my second pregnancy. I found it most disconcerting to have to call my husband to reverse into a huge parking space! It turns out that it's entirely normal as your spatial awareness also takes a break for a while. I suppose it's to allow all your senses and energies to be devoted to your baby's needs.

The days and weeks after birth you absolutely need to be pampered – your body has taken a battering; your whole world has been turned upside down. Babies don't come with a manual and you'll be bombarded with other people's advice as to what's best for you both. If it's your first, you'll be busy learning a whole load of new skills and feeling your way along. It may be wonderful, but it's still stressful. You will be exhausted, tearful and apprehensive. The Baby Blues are common in the first few weeks.

What if you're really feeling down and all manner of 'smoothies' and tender loving care won't help? Feeling out of sorts is entirely normal but if you start to feel seriously out of control, totally depressed or even suicidal, that's clearly not.

# Post-natal depression (PND)

I feel very fortunate not to have experienced PND. I think the closest I came was after my fourth baby's birth. I was exhausted beyond all description. We had very little childcare, three other children to look after and I started to feel tearful and unable to cope. I couldn't sleep even when the baby was asleep and would lie there having what felt like nightmares while I was awake. I immediately sought help and got some serious pampering. I also hugely upped my intake of essential fatty acids and drank lots of water. I went for brisk walks in the fresh air with the baby strapped to me in a sling and called upon friends and virtual friends for constant support. This wasn't PND and fortunately it passed after a few days.

I have interviewed various celebrities over the years on Radio 2 who have made their PND experiences public. It's easy for us to think that someone who seems to have it all could not possibly be affected but, as Ruby Wax said, PND is not a faddy 'feeling sorry for yourself hissy fit'. It's an illness and it doesn't care who it takes prisoner.

PND can start at any time up to about six months after the baby is born but it's most common before week four. It affects about one in ten women, but often those who suffer still perceive themselvs as odd and experience guilt for feeling miserable and overwhelmed at a time when they should feel only joy and gratitude for a healthy baby.

Interestingly, antenatal depression can occur too but sometimes goes undiagnosed. This is unfortunate as it can impact on the birth and the feelings immediately afterwards.

The bottom line is, be gentle on yourself and seek all the help you need. Lauren, one of my friends, was offered antidepressants for her PND, declined them and asked for counselling instead. Her advice is that a listening ear is worth a shed load of medication, so find someone to talk to. If you don't feel you want to see a

counsellor, get yourself some virtual support. There is lots of it around, including the parenting section on my own forum and you'll find more websites in the Directory (see page 212).

Many women are tempted to take anti-depressants if the doctor offers to prescribe them but I'd suggest it's worth trying just about everything else before you go down that route. Take advice though because, sometimes, even imperfectly natural old me has to recognise that medication really is needed to help break the spiral. Obviously, I'd recommend that if you are breastfeeding, you continue to do so as this will help to provide more uplifting hormones. Therapeutic essential oils can be extremely beneficial but this may not be a time when you will feel like mixing your own, so you can buy ready-made ones such as 'Moods' from **www.tortue rouge.co.uk**.

Consult a homeopath and consider upping your intake of Omega 3 and vitamin B. Low levels of vitamin B12 can trigger depression. There are other natural supplements to help with depression including Kava Kava and St John's Wort but both can have contra-indications, which you must check if you're breastfeeding.

One more thing that will help, although it sounds almost too simplistic to say, is to get out for a walk every single day.

# Breastfeeding

### Why breastfeed?
### (Mummy knows breast!)

Breast milk must be one of the most amazing foodstuffs known to man. Not only is it top of the nutrition charts (more on that later) but it's free and as green as you can get. It requires no additives, preservatives, bottles or packaging, fuel resources or storage and it produces no environmentally unfriendly waste.

Breast milk is a living food, designed to match exactly the individual requirements of your baby at each and every stage of his early development. What is more, it constantly changes its chemical nature, not only over days and weeks but on an hourly basis, tailoring itself to your baby's rhythms and needs throughout each day. And it's delivered at exactly the right temperature. You can't buy anything to rival it.

I don't want to boss anyone about though. Everyone's breastfeeding experiences are different and it can be a very emotive topic. For some it's painfully difficult, for others it's very easy. For all manner of reasons some will want to, but can't and others can, but won't. All I'll say is listen to your intuition, and ask yourself 'Shouldn't I at least give this my best shot?'

## What's in breast milk?

Actually, more than we know! Many in he scientific community agree that we're not completely sure of everything it contains, much to the annoyance of formula manufacturers, I suspect.

In the first few days after birth you produce colostrum, a marvellous mix of protein and antibodies that will help build your baby's resistance to infections and the growth of organisms like bacteria and viruses. Formula milk does not contain the antibodies that are in breast milk and, in my view, this is a major worry. Statistics show formula-fed babies have more incidences of hospitalisation and infection than do breastfed babies.

Your milk changes as your baby grows and you will notice the different colours and consistencies as this happens. The foods you eat will have an effect on the taste of the milk to your baby and may attune his palate to accept a wider range of flavours and tastes, potentially reducing fussiness over foods later on. You might also notice that certain foods disagree with your baby.

## Convenience

Breast milk is always fresh and always there, at exactly the right temperature. So there's no getting up in the middle of the night to warm bottles and no getting caught out when you're on the move. And don't worry if you're involving carers – the expressing and freezing procedure is simple. Feeding in public is just fine and you can be discreet. Don't let anyone tell you off for it! It's the most natural thing in the world – I've even fed mine in a pod on the London Eye!

## Skin contact

Breastfeeding is a marvellous bonding experience and has been known to help with post-birth blues (see post-natal depression, page 19). There is also research linking breastfeeding with lower risks of breast and ovarian cancer and protection against an array of health problems including diabetes, obesity, eczema, asthma, allergies, dental problems and SIDS (Sudden Infant Death Syndrome). It may even make our babies brainier! Studies suggest that IQ is higher among breastfed children.

It's well documented that premature babies and those in special-care units thrive better on expressed breast milk than they do on formula and, fortunately, there are milk banks in some hospitals and more being set up. They can and do save lives and I'd encourage you to donate your milk if you find you have too much. If you're concerned by the possibility of infection, by the way, all the human milk is pasteurised and, in any case, donors are screened for HIV and other infections. For more information, go to **www.ukamb.org**.

## How to breastfeed

Most mothers are able to breastfeed. Even with problems like inverted nipples or after breast surgery it can still be possible, though more challenging. In the case of breast reduction, much depends on the amount of surgical damage done to the milk ducts around the nipple. There is some excellent help at **www.bfar.org**.

Immediately after birth, your baby will instinctively want to feed and your midwife will help you to encourage him to latch on correctly and establish skin-to-skin contact. This is vitally important in the moments after birth. The period has been called the 'golden hour' and you should not let the midwife take your baby away to be washed or weighed too quickly.

Most problems with breastfeeding arise because of poor positioning or because the baby is not latched on correctly. After you get home, you may be in a bit of a daze and may forget what you have been shown, so here are some tips.

Your baby and you should be comfortable. Sit up reasonably straight. In the early weeks you may find it helpful to have a breastfeeding cushion. Let your baby turn his whole body towards you (his head shouldn't be tilted too much) and let him latch on by encouraging him to open his mouth wide. I found I could do this by gently touching his cheek and upper lip with my nipple. He needs to get a mouthful of the whole areola to latch on correctly. Make sure he doesn't just suckle the end of your nipple as, not only does it hurt like hell after a while, but he won't get much milk either. Generally speaking, although the first few feeds may make your eyes water a bit, breastfeeding should not give you any pain or discomfort at all.

Should you offer both breasts at each feed? Well, it took me two babies to get to grips with this one. I was swinging the baby from boob to boob for months; the poor mite must have been dizzy. Finally, someone pointed out to me that it's best to let him have a good long feed on one breast, emptying it if possible, and then top up with the other if needed. Obviously, you'll need to alternate sides with each feed. If you can't tell which side is the heavier, get

yourself a fun 'next boob' bracelet to wear on the corresponding wrist (see breast-feeding kit). The milk, wondrous as it is, changes during the feed and your baby needs to get both the foremilk, which will satisfy his thirst, and the hind milk which is rich in nutrients. Swapping to the other breast may not apply if, as in my case, you have a baby on one boob and a toddler on the other! Come to think of it, I may have swapped them both around at the same time for fun. If you're feeding from one breast, you'll often find the other one leaks, so it's a great idea to catch the drips in a breast shell or later on express from one breast while you're feeding from the other. Don't try this until breastfeeding is well established, however.

Forget about timing the feeds. Whoever said that was necessary? Let your baby lead the way. He will let you know when he's hungry. I fed on demand and instinctively knew it was the natural thing to do. Even in the middle of the night I found I could manage fine by lying on my side, half asleep with the baby in bed with me suckling contentedly. Feeding a baby on demand and even through the night is considerably less stressful than wandering down to the kitchen to heat a bottle of formula to take to a crying baby in another room. Breastfeeding really is the easy option.

When your baby's finished, he may simply fall asleep while latched on. Insert your little finger (clean) gently into the corner of his mouth and he'll pop away from your breast – until next time, which may be only twenty minutes later – there really is no routine in the early weeks. As time goes on, breastfeeding will become second nature to you and you'll learn all the tricks as you go.

## Muslin squares

In the first few weeks the only 'scarves' you'll need are muslin squares, so buy lots of them. Some people call them 'burp cloths' (charming!) and they also make excellent nappies for newborns.

## Pillows

There are lots of breastfeeding pillows on the market including tripillows and circular ones that work by providing support for the baby's head. To be honest, after a couple of weeks I found I didn't use it. If you've got bigger boobs though, you do need good breast support while nursing.

The 'Utterly Yours Breast Pillow' comes in three sizes and costs about £17. You can also buy the 'epi-pillow' for perineal discomfort and the other very popular breastfeeding pillow, worth it for the name alone, is the 'My Breast Friend'. It has a firm base, wraps around and can be secured. It has a handy pocket for a muslin square and, best of all, it supports your back. Visit **www.babydayz.co.uk**.

## Problems

All in all, I've been lucky, though I've had a few problems, mainly with my breasts becoming engorged when I went back to work. I was relying on expressed milk to feed the baby but was slightly pushing it on the number of hours I was away from home. The truth is, it's sometimes not all plain sailing and problems may crop up. If you need to talk to someone, there are several organisations that will give you free help and advice. There are trained counsellors, who have all breastfed themselves, available on the end of a telephone. Some will even come out and sit with you to help you get the positioning right. These are dedicated women and the services they offer are brilliant, and free of charge.

The ABM
(Association of
Breastfeeding
Mothers):
**www.abm.me.uk**
La Leche League:
**www.laleche.org.uk**
NCT: **www.nctpregnancy
andbabycare.com**
The Breastfeeding Network:
**www.breastfeedingnetwork.org.uk**
There's lots more information at
**www.breastfeeding.com**

# I♥mperfectly natural parent

**Your name, age group, age of children** Sarah Barnard, 37, kids now 6 and 3.

**Occupation?** Prior to my first child, I was a shop manager for a large retail chain. After my second child, I set up www.ethics trading.com.

**Birth experiences – natural/assisted?** Both births were natural. The first was long, with three weeks of slow labour ending in exhaustion for us both. The second was relaxed and wonderful. I used minimal pain relief with both.

**Did the baby's birth impact in any way on the first few weeks – positively or negatively?** YES! Both times there was an impact. First time I was exhausted and sore – the baby refused to latch on properly and his face was so bruised and swollen it was hard for him to feed. The second time was very different. It was a relaxed labour and birth. She fed within minutes and carried on for 23 months.

**Your emotional state for the first six months?** With my son (R), I returned to work and was tired but OK. After my daughter (M), I was diagnosed with post-natal depression. I know that having children has changed me emotionally. I don't look at things the same way any more. There are films I used to watch over and over that I now can't watch at all.

**Your physical health?** R was OP presentation and did some damage to my coccix as he came out. My back hasn't recovered yet and probably never will. As a result of weight loss after his birth, I discovered I have a mild heart condition. Since M was born, I have downsized our lives and as a result our overall health is vastly improved.

**When did your figure return? Did you exercise?** I was back in my pre-pregnancy jeans six days after having R and 10 days after having M. Actually I had trouble keeping weight on after R was born.

**How was your relationship with your partner?** My partner and I split up.

**Breastfeeding experience?** With R it was the hardest thing I did. My nipples were cracked and bleeding. We both got thrush and he seemed constantly hungry. There was no real support and at four months he cut a tooth and started chewing me! It was just too painful. M was completely different. She latched on easily and fed on demand. I had huge amounts of support from my local Surestart (www.surestart. gov.uk/). They got me through the growth spurts, M being ill and the PND. M fed until she chose to give up at 23 months.

**Nappies – if cloth, which type do your prefer and why?** CLOTH! I was a Lollipop (www.teamlollipop. co.uk) advisor for a few years. I used a combination of Sandy's, Tots bots, Terry squares and some wraps.

**First foods – homemade purées or jars?** M refused to eat anything that didn't come out of a jar at one point. So I used to make my own and decant it into a jar.

**Over the age of one – what does your child eat frequently?** Mine are the kids that will ask for a carrot for a snack. They love homemade soup with homemade bread.

**Junk food/sweets?** Hmm, they do like fast-food outlets but I suspect it's because of the toys they get. I do try to keep sweets to a minimum but Green and Black's chocolate is sooo yummy.

**What's in your medicine cupboard for the kids?**
I have a Helios homeopathy kit (**www.helios. co.uk**) and I find it's great for all of us. I have plasters, cotton wool and an antiseptic spray – but it's tea tree and lavender from Amphora Aromatics (**www. amphora-aromatics.com**).

**What do you do to keep 'sane'? What do you do for 'me' time?** My big sanity saver is my writing. I started writing as a way of coping with splitting up with my partner of 16 years. I finished my first novel in five months and sent it off to a publisher.

**What is your favourite holistic treatment/ therapy?** I love aromatherapy. I usually have a candle or oil burner on. I also have a BIOFlow bracelet that seems to help keep my back under control.

**Sleep (or lack of)?** I don't sleep enough. I go to bed late. It's often 2 a.m. before I pull my head out of writing and decide I should get some sleep.

**Skincare – soaps, moisturisers, sunscreen?** We wash with the most innocuous products we can find locally. Actually, a bag of soap nuts hung under the hot tap while running a bath adds a bit of saponin to the bath and no other soap is needed.

**How do you deal with challenging behaviour?** Mine or the kids? With the kids, I try to reason and explain why something isn't acceptable but I don't always succeed. I use time out to try to get anyone to calm down before they get too angry.

**As a family, how green are you? 10 is dark and leafy, 1 is a faint hint of peppermint.** As the owner of a business called Ethics Trading, I should be able to say 10, shouldn't I? But no, I am human. I'm probably a 6.

**Do you recycle everything?** All cardboard, paper, tins, cans, glass and garden waste – yes. If it's not composted we have a roadside collection. I don't recycle plastic through pure laziness, I'm afraid.

**Do you consider fair-trade/ethical trading?** All the time. I prefer to give my custom to a business that is ethical and transparent in its dealings. My children are aware of certain brands that we avoid on principle.

**What's your top ten eco-family tip?** DIY. Do it yourself. Compost and use it on your garden, reuse packaging as gift wrap, fit your own grey waste water collection system for watering the garden.

**What are your favourite simple activities to do with babies ?** Snuggling, I love snuggling babies!

**Toddlers?** Things that involve getting messy. Digging in the garden, playing with clay, playdough, paint.

**How much TV do you/will you allow your child to watch?** They get about half an hour in the evenings – it helps calm them down while I cook tea.

**Your top three tips for imperfectly natural parenting?** Be with your children. Enjoy every second you have with them. Rediscover that simple joy that kids have.

**Parenting pleasures – what do you most love about being a mum? What are your imperfections?** I adore the comments they make and the questions they ask. Their laughter is better than any antidepressant, more potent than sunshine. I do stash sweets for me and I have been known to raid their chocolates. I know I shout more than I should.

**Anything else you'd like to share to help towards an imperfectly natural world?** Today, after you read this, try to smile at a stranger, hug a friend and pay an unexpected compliment. The feel-good factor is huge, for everyone. We can all make a small difference.

# Not enough milk

Many women worry about this and some give up breast feeding because they are worried their baby isn't getting enough nourishment. If you are healthy, well fed, getting enough rest yourself and the baby is growing normally, it may be less of a problem than you think. Don't be concerned with optimum weight charts. This information is often based on data relating to formula-fed babies and may not necessarily apply to breastfed infants. Formula milk is less easily digestible and as a result, formula-fed babies can weigh more.

If your baby is producing five or so wet nappies a day and a few bowel movements in a twenty-four hour period, it's a good indication that he's feeding well. Check that the meconium (sticky dark initial bowel movements) does not continue beyond four or five days and that he's into regular, lighter movements of a more watery nature. Stools can vary greatly in shade from green to mustard, so don't be alarmed by variations in colour and texture. If your baby is gaining weight, it is a fairly good indication that he's getting enough milk.

If your baby cries after a feed, there could be issues involving correct latching on, colic, or maybe he just needs longer on the breast (don't time him!). Mothers who worry about not having enough milk often decide to give top-up feeds with formula milk. Take a few days to assess the situation before you go down this route. It may be that you need to feed more frequently to boost your own milk supply. Make sure you're getting really good nutrition yourself and lots of water and, most importantly, plenty of rest as this greatly affects supply. If your baby still seems to be hungry, it may be a little growth spurt and it will settle down in a day or so. I went through this with one of my sons but, after calming down, I had a small glass of Guinness (I read the advice of another imperfect mother who said it boosted milk supply) and just lived with it. We settled back into a regular pattern quite easily. If you really think your baby is distressed as a result of hunger, seek advice.

## Sore and cracked nipples

It is fairly common for nipples to get sore and cracked, and even to bleed. This can be really painful and is one of the main reasons why some women give up breastfeeding. If you have this problem, check that your baby is latching on correctly, not just on to the nipple. It's easy to think you've got the positioning completely right when in fact the angle of the baby's head may not be quite right and he may be dragging the breast down. I can't stress enough the need to call in help. Don't be afraid to admit you're getting it wrong, after all it's not easy to see yourself as you're looking down. Someone else, even your partner or a friend, can bend down in front of you and see if the baby is positioned correctly and the mouth is wide open.

A little olive oil may help and you should let the air get to your nipples if you can. I personally don't like any of the regular over-the-counter creams for sore nipples, preferring instead to rub breast milk around the whole area. It's wonderfully healing.

If your nipples are really sore, ridiculous though it may seem, try to keep feeding. If you really can't manage it, then hand-express a little milk from the worst affected nipple and feed with the other one for a while.

## Engorged breasts and mastitis

If you build up a pattern of regular breastfeeding, your breasts will tailor the amount of milk they produce to the demand. It all works fine until you stop. Suddenly having to spend an unusual amount of time away from your baby will mean your breasts may become heavy with milk and possibly engorged and you'll need either to get back to your baby quickly, or find a way of expressing the milk.

You must deal with engorged breasts as they can become very painful and potentially lead to mastitis. The Bowen Technique can help with this (page 165). I've already mentioned the cabbage leaf and comb trick that I found worked for me (see Breasts, page 16). Mastitis is one stage further on when you may have a reddening on the breast or even what feels like a hard lump. You may suffer flu-like symptoms and feel really miserable for a couple of days. The worry is that it's an inflammation of the breast and may become infected but, unless a doctor advises that it's essential for you, try to avoid antibiotics. The best thing you can do is take to your bed with the baby and feed more! Drink lots of fluids and massage the breasts regularly.

If you have any minor illness, the advice is much the same, just continue to breastfeed as much as possible. When I had a vomiting bug when Lulu was about two weeks old, I was terrified that I would be passing all my horrible germs into her but I rang the Association of Breastfeeding Mothers who reassured me that my own antibodies in the breast milk would protect the baby. I carried on breastfeeding while feeling terrible and, although Lulu chucked back her milk a few times, she seemed absolutely fine. If you are more seriously ill and need to go to hospital, you should still be allowed to have your baby brought to you to feed if you are able. You could build up a store of expressed milk over time so you won't feel so panicky if, for whatever reason, you need to miss out a few feeds.

If your baby is poorly, the message is the same: feed him as much as he seems to want. The scary time is when you can't seem to get a baby interested in feeding at all. If they are too sleepy or don't want to feed, express your milk frequently to keep your milk supply going and, of course, get professional advice.

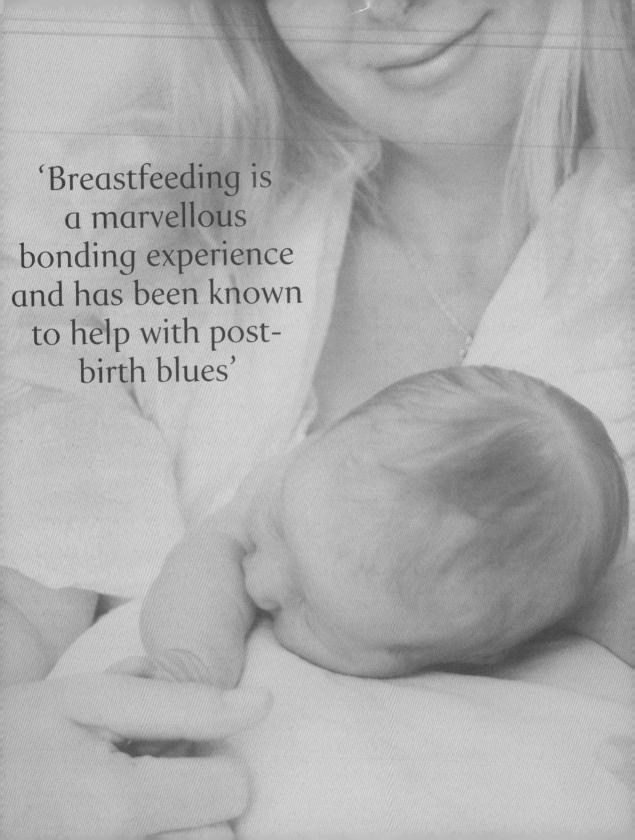

'Breastfeeding is a marvellous bonding experience and has been known to help with post-birth blues'

## Thrush

Thrush can be a miserable condition to treat and will usually present in both the baby's mouth and around the mother's nipples. I've never experienced it, but I'm told it can be really sore and makes feeding very painful. Sometimes it's caused by antibiotics taken to treat an infection (ironic, isn't it?). Be scrupulous about cleaning bottles and teats. You'll need to see a doctor and may have to use anti-fungal cream or take tablets. It's worth trying the homeopathic remedies Borax 30c and Candida 30c alternately every three hours for a few days. Remove dairy and sugar from your diet too. The important thing is to keep feeding!

## Expressing milk

I knew from the start that I intended to go back to work after my first baby was born, albeit only for a few hours a couple of days a week, but I was keen to make sure that my baby would be happy with expressed milk. I made the mistake of buying a battery-operated expresser and trying it on about day five. It hurt like hell and I got the tiniest dribble of milk. I'm a bit wiser now and realise that it's not a good idea to try expressing milk until a good breastfeeding pattern is established at around six weeks. Before then, it's confusing for your milk supply, which doesn't know if it's meant to be meeting the seemingly endlessly changing needs of

the tiny newborn or the pump which demands yet more. I would say though, feel free to hand express a little milk if you can get the hang of that and also collect all your leaked milk in breast shells. Most aren't discreet enough to wear while you're out (you'll have to lose the precious extra milk to the breast pad), but while I was at home I walked around with boobs hugely extended wearing breast shells.

Once you get on to expressing, there are many different pumps and I think I tried them all. Many women love the Avent hand pump and you can get them any-where. I couldn't get on with any of the hand or battery types apart from one really old-fashioned one called a 'breast reliever' that looked a bit like a tiny car horn with a kind of rubber ball attached to a plastic cup that fits over the breast. With one hand you just squeeze the pump gently and collect the milk. Most professionals probably wouldn't recommend them because the rubber bit means they cannot be put into an electric steriliser. I just used to wash mine immediately after use in boiling hot water and regularly use a sterilising fluid, and had no problems. The other advantage is that they are entirely silent. You can order them from the pharmacy at Tesco. Just ask for a 'breast reliever' which costs around £10.

I could only ever express while my baby was feeding from the other breast so it would have been hopeless for me to try to express while away from the baby. Many women manage to overcome this by taking a photo of their baby or even a tape of him crying to stimulate the milk flow when the baby isn't around.

When I had my second baby, I was tandem-feeding and found it hard to keep up the milk supply, so I invested in a hospital-style industrial electric pump. Initially, I hired one from a local NCT counsellor for a couple of pounds a week. After I'd done that for a while I decided to buy one. I was concerned that the domestic versions wouldn't be as good, but I needn't have worried as the twin pump I bought from Ameda Lactaline Personal is fantastic. It's very quiet and works both on batteries and mains (**www.nctms.co.uk**).

## Storing and freezing breast milk

You'll need to store the milk, once expressed, in a sterile container. It will keep for a few hours at room temperature, a few days in the fridge but up to six months in the freezer, so always be sure to date your milk and set up a system. It's a good idea to thaw and reheat it using hot water in a bowl or in a bottle warmer. Don't take it to boiling point and never microwave it. Do swirl it around once it is thawed as the creamy bit tends to separate. One thing that may freak you out when you start using expressed breast milk is how it looks. Mine had a distinct green tinge one day, but it was just because I'd been eating lots of green leafy veg. If you taste it, you can get a shock too. It's usually very sweet but with an underlying weird, almost metallic taste. I remember posting lots of panicky messages about this on internet support group sites but I was always assured that, as long as it has been stored correctly, it's fine. For information and support, go to **www.babygroe.co.uk**.

The logistics of freezing breast milk can drive you bonkers! You'll be going great guns for a while then one day you'll find you have a good supply of milk and want to freeze some. Either you'll have run out of freezer bags (and they're hideously expensive) or you'll fill a nice big bag, and when it's defrosted, the baby will take only a tiny amount and you will have to throw the rest away.

Breast milk storage bags are tiny little sterile plastic freezer bags that, with any luck, when defrosted will fit into most bottles. I must say, after the first three babies, I got fed up with buying them at around £8 a box and used my regular small sandwich bags positioned in a bottle lid in the freezer to freeze them into the right shape.

If you are going to use milk storage bags, try to get the additive- and plasticiser-free ones. You can get them from **www.spiritof nature.co.uk** for about £5 but, personally, I prefer 'milk trays'. They're far more eco-friendly than regular plastic sterile bags, cost

around £20 for two trays with lids and take up far less room in the freezer (**www.maternityandnursing.co.uk**).

## Long-term breastfeeding

How long should you breastfeed for? The answer is for as long as your baby and you are both okay with it. I am a fan of long-term breastfeeding but, more to the point, I am a believer in baby-led breastfeeding. I'd say categorically don't make it less than six months but after that, see what happens.

The common misconception is that toddlers who are breastfed don't eat any food and are constantly hanging from the boob. This isn't the case. All of my toddlers, once past a certain age, seemed instinctively to under-stand that 'booby' is for at home. I fed Sonny for just over two years, tandem-fed Buddy and then got utterly exhausted and stopped at fifteen months. As I write, I am still feeding Lulu, aged fourteen months. I don't know when my cut-off point will be as I trust my instinct. Never stop breastfeeding just because someone else says you should but, by the same token, don't continue because of some need of your own either. Some women stop once the baby bites but do try to ride it out. Yes, it hurts like hell, but a firm 'no' and removing the baby immediately usually gets the message across. Night-time feeding puts women off too and, if feeding on demand means fifteen times during the night, it's exhausting and, in truth, not usually essential by the time a baby is over six months old.

However, with their totally different body clocks and the fact that they are growing at a tremendous rate, some babies really are hungry after sleeping for about four hours. The difficulty is determining whether a baby or toddler is waking and crying for food because he is actually hungry, or just for comfort. The No-Cry Sleep Solution (See Recommended Reading, page 210) is an excellent book to help you through this one (see also pages 72–82).

Let's conclude by saying breast is best, for the baby and for you. Breastfeeding has many advantages for the mother's health, including reduced susceptibility to certain cancers and a delay in the return of their periods. That, in turn, can mean delayed menopause and its associated risk of osteoporosis. It is important to state that whether your periods return fairly quickly, or take months after having a baby, you should not rely on breastfeeding or lack of menstruation as a sign that you are not able to conceive.

## Formula-feeding

It will come as no surprise to you that I am not a fan of formula milk. Most regular brands contain sugar or some form of sweetener. If you do choose or have to bottle feed or when breastfeeding ends, you'll need to find a formula milk that suits your baby. We all know that ordinary cow's milk is indigestible for babies under a year (many people would argue at any age) and most formulas are based on this, so what else can you give? I know several people who use goat's milk formula and one mother who gives her nine-month-old twins organic goat's milk mixed with a little water. I'd try to find an organic infant formula milk. Many of the brands that make baby foods such as Holle (**www.ulula.co.uk**) and Hipp are available in most supermarkets. Babynat cow and goat's organic formula is sold in some health shops and you can get it from **www.goodnessdirect.co.uk**. As a follow-on milk there's also buffalo milk which is said to be much easier to digest and, as the buffalo is unaltered by genetic manipulation, they can still thrive without the need for antibiotics and high-protein feeds. The milk is

HIGHLY RECOMMENDED BOOKS
Breastfeeding: The Essential Guide by Sharon Trotter, Midwife and Mother (Trotters Independent Publishing Services)
The Breastfeeding Book: Everything You Need to Know About Nursing Your Child from Birth Through Weaning by Martha Sears and M.D. William Sears (Little, Brown)
NCT Breastfeeding for Beginners by Caroline Deacon (HarperCollins)

significantly lower in cholesterol and higher in calcium than cow's, sheep's or goat's and, unlike the array of industrially produced soya and other cereal milk, it is totally free of additives and chemical formulations. It's very hard to get hold of in Europe but you can buy it from some branches of Waitrose. There are other buffalo products available too such as ice cream, cheese and yoghurt (**www. buffalomilk. co.uk**).

Make sure you check out a variety of bottles. There are lots of different teats available. Some are intended to mimic the nipple with several tiny suction holes rather than just one.

'My baby won't take a bottle' is a cry you hear quite often. I must admit I was so determined that mine would have no problem that I introduced them all to a bottle quite early on. In retrospect, I think it was a bad idea because it can lead to confusion between opening the mouth wide for a nipple and pursing the lips together to suck from a teat. It's best to wait until feeding is well established at six weeks or so. From around four months you can offer a cup.

# Bras

This one is a bottomless (or topless) pit. It's totally individual and depends on the size of your boobs, what type of bra you normally wear and how much you want to spend. Don't get these confused with maternity bras, which are for the pregnancy stage as your breasts grow. Nursing bras are usually fairly regular bras but they have different fastenings to drop down the cup for feeding.

Because I've got fairly small boobs, if I'm not pregnant or feeding, I don't usually wear tight-fitting bras. I also buy into the theory that underwired bras are extremely bad for you if worn regularly. I prefer a sporty-type nursing bra so, for me, the Bravado is brilliant. You can get them in a wide range of sizes, in a flowery design, leopard print, or just plain black or white. They look like workout bras rather than underwear and you can wear them under a skimpy top in summer (**www.bravadodesigns.co.uk**).

Many breastfeeding bras are opened by unhooking the straps but I find a popper works better and the Bravado bra is really

easy to undo. A similar but cheaper option is the nursing bra from **www.maternity andnursing.co.uk** that comes in a range of plain colours and sizes ranging from 32B to 52H.

You may be shocked to find that, for the first few weeks of breastfeeding, it can be a real effort to get yourself fully dressed (or is it just me?). There have been many occasions when the postman has rung the doorbell and been greeted with at least one displayed boob (by accident, I assure you). There was also a time when I was determined to get out to a natural parent group and finally got out of the door. Once in the car, heading out of the drive and feeling harassed, I checked the mirror and I realised I was wearing nothing but palazzo pants and a nursing bra! So my personal choice is to go for a bra which, on occasion, can be the only thing I wear up top, whether absent-mindedly or by design.

If you are a designer-underwear kind of girl, you'll be delighted with the very pretty but also practical Elle Macpherson range. You can get them and most other good bras at **www.expressyourselfmums.co.uk** and from all good department stores, some of which have a free fitting service. I suggest you get at least three nursing bras.

## Breast pads

Most mothers find initially that their nipples will leak a fair bit so you'll need breast pads. I highly recommend the washable ones. Disposable are obviously more readily available but, apart from the fact that they're expensive, they'll add yet more to the landfill site and before they disintegrate, they will leave your boobs feeling really sticky. Buy yourself lots of washable pads. The nicest I've found are the organic cotton ones from Lasinoh (**www.lasinoh.co.uk**).

You should also get some breast shells that will collect the milk for freezing to top up expressed milk feeds later. The ones I used were pretty hard and uncomfortable to wear but you can now get ventilated soft cushion breast shields from Avent (**www.avent.com**).

If you get the opportunity to dress up, the last thing you want is leaking nipples or visible breast pads. This is the time to invest in some LilyPadz, a truly wonderful invention that kind of sticks over your breast and stop your nipples from leaking. You can get them from **www.maternity andnursing.co.uk**.

## What to wear in public

I avoided the specially designed breast-feeding shirts and tried a long denim style shirt with a flap over the boob that you were meant to flip up to feed the baby, but it felt bizarre. I soon realised that all I needed was an easy-access top. Avoid dresses, obviously. I found waist-length

T-shirts were best. Avoid light-coloured plain tops or you get that awful dark wet patch when your boobs leak. Now I wear a fairly low top that I can pull down under the boob and a scarf that I chuck over my exposed shoulder. If you feel you do need special nursing tops, the best I've seen are two-layered tops from **www.babydayz. co.uk**. Also, there are the rather ingenious Bebe au Lait nursing covers that are made of a lightweight fabric in a range of colours. They fit over your head so that your whole boob and below is covered but you can still see your baby. There's a terry towelling section that's great for wiping and they can double as a lightweight blanket or a sunshade over a buggy. Again, these are from **www.maternityand nursing.co.uk**

## Fab stuff to buy

You can make breastfeeding fun by treating yourself to a few funky pro-breastfeeding T-shirts from **www.lactivist. co.uk**. Mine says 'I like milk from my mum, not from just any old cow'. They also do badges, bags and fabric shopping bags that say 'Mummy Milk Rocks!'

To jazz up any T-shirt and give your baby something to play with, you must treat yourself to a nursing necklace. One of the delights of feeding my fourth baby is that I've finally discovered Jingleboobs. Now, before you panic and wonder what on earth I'm doing with my bosoms in public,

Jingleboobs are bright and funky nursing beads that jingle and are designed to be strong enough for the baby to pull at while feeding. To go with them, Mandy of Jingleboobs fame also makes little nursing beaded bracelets. You can get them personalised with your baby's name and the idea is to switch them to the wrist that corresponds with the next breast you'll be offering. After the early months when your breasts no longer get really full, it's very easy to forget. My little coloured bracelet says 'Lulu's next boob', and it gets a great reaction from the guys at work (**www.lait damour.com**).

## 'Belly huggers'

One of the most useful things I found when I was very aware of my 'baby belly' (still am actually) was the 'belly hugger'. I can rarely find trousers that come up to my waist and I don't want to wear long tops (in case I want to go up and under, as it were), so what do I need? A belly hugger – great for anyone with a bit of a spare tyre or builder's bum that they want to cover. They aren't very tight fitting or corset-like as the name might suggest, just a stretchy bit of fabric approximately ten inches deep that fits around your waist and hips. They come in various colours and just look like an extension of the T-shirt or top you're wearing. I couldn't live without mine. They cost approximately £10 from **www.maternityandnursing. co.uk**.

## Nappies

Before we get on to the specifics of nappy types, let's just for one second consider the process of changing your baby's nappy. I had never so much as been near a nappy until I changed my baby about three hours after his birth. When, on the few occasions friends with babies came to visit, I would make myself scarce when the nappy-change moment arrived. There are still many fathers who pride themselves on never having changed a nappy, yet what I'm about to say may surprise you – changing your baby's nappy can be an incredibly rewarding experience. I know you're thinking I must be at best a little odd but, truthfully, it's a wonderful opportunity to connect with your baby and make eye contact. It's an opportunity to massage them, talk to them and nurture them. Try to make it a dignified bonding time for the baby and, by the way, the safest place to change them is on a mat on the floor. You definitely don't need a changing table.

In a nutshell, there are two routes you can go – disposables or washables. (Washables? I hear you scream, she must be joking!) But when I tell you about them, you'll soon see that it's not such a scary idea. What you might find scary is what I shall tell you about what's in most disposables; the substances that can leach not only into the environment but into your baby's skin and what the long-term effects of that could be.

## Disposables

We know that many chemicals can be absorbed into the body via the skin and, as a baby's skin is so much thinner and more delicate, I was worried about putting a load of synthetic chemical gel so close to the skin. For starters, the bleach that's used on the outer and inner material of disposables is thought by some to produce the chemical Dioxin which is a known carcinogen. Solvents and other chemicals that are used to make them super absorbent have also been associated with health risks. There were concerns in the 1980s over similar chemicals used in tampons and linked with the development of 'toxic shock syndrome'.

In baby boys, a great wad of paper and stuffing also increases the temperature around the testicles. The male reproductive system develops during the first two years of life and it's widely known that high scrotal temperature can be a factor in low sperm count. (I used disposables on my first two boys. Can you see me beating myself up?)

A study by the Women's Environmental Network about seven years ago included a chemical analysis of five types of newborn nappies. Each contained small amounts of tributylin, a type of chemical that can disrupt immune cells. Their study showed that babies, with their underdeveloped immune systems, could be exposed on a

'Changing your baby's nappy can be an incredibly rewarding experience'

daily basis to 3.6 times the World Health Organisation's estimated tolerable level. The real truth is that we don't know the effects of disposable nappies on the skin or how any traces of these chemicals affect our babies if they travel internally. It's certainly unlikely that the substances are helping in the fight against eczema and allergies, infertility or even cancer.

From an environmental standpoint, in Britain alone we throw away eight million nappies every day, making up over four per cent of landfill domestic waste. Every one of them could take 200 to 500 years to decompose fully. Consider also the fact that human faeces are classified as clinical waste and, as such, should be incinerated. At one time, everyone was fully aware of this and always put the poo in the loo. Now, for some reason, disposable nappy packs no longer carry the warning that solid waste should be disposed of down the toilet. Tests have shown that up to one hundred viruses can be present in human faeces, with the added risk that viruses and bacteria will leach into rivers and find their way back into the food chain.

## The alternatives to disposables

Firstly, let's be imperfectly natural here and talk about some of the more eco-friendly disposables on the market. These are made by companies who seem more aware of the potential health implications for your baby, as well as the environmental issues

posed by use of regular disposables. We'll get greener with the washables later!

Moltex Oko nappies have won a number of awards in their native Germany, itself a highly environmentally aware country. They're bleach-free, so they're off-white in colour and we're promised that they contain reduced chemicals, no latex, perfumes, or antioxidants. You can buy Moltex Oko nappies from some health food shops, or by mail order from **www.spiritofnature.co.uk**.

There is also the Nature Boy and Girl nappy from Sweden. The outer layer is made from GM-free maize starch and, because of their unique design, their nappies need less of the synthetic non-biodegradable super-absorbent material. Fortunately, you can get them in Sainsbury's.

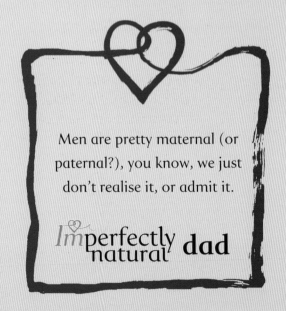

Men are pretty maternal (or paternal?), you know, we just don't realise it, or admit it.

Imperfectly natural **dad**

Tushies make disposable nappies that claim to be completely gel-free, perfume-free, dye-free and latex-free. They contain non-chlorine-bleached wood pulp. For the cotton and other whitened bits of the Tushie disposable, they use an environmentally friendly process. They are sold in some branches of Boots, health food shops and from **www.greenbaby.co.uk**. My suggestion is that you nag your local supermarkets to stock a range of eco-disposables.

## Cloth nappies

When I first heard about a neighbour who was using cloth nappies, I remember thinking 'That's fine for you; you've got all the time in the world and enough cash to hire a laundry service. I thought there was no way I would have the time or resources to deal with them and, on this issue, I decided I would remain imperfect and just accept that real nappies weren't for me. Oh, how easy it is to be ignorant!

I first came from the standpoint of what I suspected was wrong with disposables rather than what was right with washables. I wanted to avoid all the problems of landfill issues, chemicals, bleaches, and antioxidants but it took me some time to appreciate the many benefits of using washables.

Where to start? Well, it's not like the old days when a terry square, a safety pin and some plastic pants were all that was on offer. A whole industry has grown up around individual styles, shapes and designs. There are masses of different types and the old safety pin has long gone. When I first started to think about it I had no idea what a nappy nipper or an aplix fastening was. I did not know my pre-fold from my stuffables and, never having been good at origami, I was afraid it would all take far longer than just bunging on a disposable.

Fortunately, there is a huge amount of information and help available. My first point of contact was a fab website (**www.the nappylady.com**), which is worth a visit for the name alone. The nappy lady knows everything there is to know about the subject and sells every different type of nappy and associated parapher-nalia you could want. Also excellent is **www.teamlollipop.co.uk**.

So, what are the advantages? First, gone are the bleaches, gels and other chemicals that so worried me, along with the mountains of waste being absorbed into the environment. Also, cloth nappies are cheaper. If you change your baby's disposables fairly regularly, you will probably get through between four and six thousand nappies per child! You will be in for around £1,000 for disposables compared to around £400 for cloth nappies, which you can use for subsequent babies.

Putting your baby in cloth nappies almost certainly helps with toilet training. This is

# Imperfectly natural parent

**Your name, age group, age of children** Christopher, aged 32. Children: Poppy 5, Mabel 2, and one on the way.

**Occupation?** Co-owner of The Ethical Food Company.

**Birth experiences – natural/assisted?** First – watched C-section. Second – watched natural (with epidural).

**Your emotional state for the first six months?** Fine – the first one changes your life and you have to make big adjustments. The second – much easier, though more exhausting!

**Your physical health?** Mine . . . fine!

**How was your relationship with your partner?** It changed a lot – but that had a lot to do with other things. My wife had suffered with anorexia/personality disorder. The arrival of our first daughter meant my main focus was to care for the baby rather than my wife, which she found very difficult to handle and caused severe mental health problems for her.

**Breastfeeding experience?** Both children have been bottle-fed from birth, partly because of the medication issues related to my wife's health. Both fed on Aptamil and have been very healthy on it!

**First foods – homemade purées or jars?** Both have only ever been fed on homemade purees – they wouldn't ever eat bought jars after having proper food!

**Over the age of one – what do your children eat frequently?** They have both always just eaten the same foods that we eat – we always try to sit down round the table to eat together. They're great with fruit and veg (and it helps that we get good-quality food that tastes so good – they love the flavours). We even had them eating mild curries before the age of two!

**Junk food/sweets?** Very little. We don't feed them much in the way of junk food. Don't really used processed foods other than things like organic pasta sauces. Never taken them to fast-food chains. They do have sweets from time to time.

**How is their general health?** Very good. No health problems.

**What's in your medicine cupboard for the kids?** Calpol/Nurofen. Sudocreme. Piz Buin Factor 30 sun cream.

**What is your own diet like?** Reasonably healthy! A lot of organic and locally grown fresh foods. Probably too much red meat!

**What do you do to keep 'sane'? What do you do for 'me' time?** Play sports (cricket, squash) and some social time out of the home.

**What is your favourite holistic treatment/therapy?** Don't really have one! Just need music and some time for me!

**Sleep (or lack of)?** Pretty good – the girls have always been good sleepers. We consciously got them into a good, fairly strict routine early on – they're in bed 7 p.m. to 7.30 p.m. and we don't see them until 7 a.m.!

**Sex (or lack of)?** It's OK… nothing to shout about, but fine.

**Skincare – soaps, moisturisers, sunscreen?** Plenty of sunscreen for the kids.

**Haircare?** What's hair care, apart from a bit of shampoo and an occasional cut?

**How do you get exercise?** Occasional bit of sport… and walking the dog… and playing with the kids!

**How do you deal with challenging behaviour?** From the wife or the kids??!! We have always set the girls very clear boundaries for what's acceptable and not acceptable, and by and large they have not really tested them. If we do anything when one of them is playing up, we will tend to exclude them (make them sit on the stairs or in their bedroom on their own) until they are ready to come and join in and behave! Basically… ignore it and there's no point in them continuing with it!

**Do you employ childcare?** Just a wife – but she costs enough!!!

**Did you change your car when you increased your family?** Yes. To a big estate car – enough for kids/prams/dog!

**Where do you go on holiday with the children?** So far… UK, France and Spain.

**As a family, how green are you? 10 is dark and leafy, 1 is a faint hint of peppermint.** Probably 6 or 7.

**Do you recycle everything?** Pretty much – where we can.

**Do you consider fair-trade/ethical trading?** Yes – I've started The Ethical Food Company … so I'd better!

**What's your top ten eco-family tip?** I'm not a fan of supermarkets. Use local food suppliers – they are out there. Walk or use a bike wherever you can!

**What are your favourite simple activities to do with babies?** Honest answer…. not great at babies! Just to spend time with them and stimulate their minds!

**Toddlers?** Reading. Physical play/games, especially outdoors whenever possible. Simple puzzles and games. Colouring.

**How much TV do you/will you allow your child to watch?** Try for it not to be more than an hour a day, although not always successful!

**At what age do you think 'screens' are OK?** TV from an early age can be very stimulating for a baby and entertaining and educational for older children – depends on what they watch. I won't allow my kids to have a TV in their own room though. Computers? They do use them now at an early age, but again, only for a short time and on certain good websites.

**Your top three tips for imperfectly natural parenting?** Set really clear boundaries for what's acceptable and what's not… then stick to them! Be prepared to make sacrifices to your own lifestyle to spend time with your kids, doing kids' things and enjoy the time you get with them. Accept that you can't always get everything right… just try your best.

**Parenting pleasures – what do you most love about being dad? What are your imperfections?** Seeing your kids happy and laughing – there is nothing in the world that gives you the same feeling!

**Do you keep all the balls in the air? If not, why not? Is it lack of time?** I try, but let's face it, we all drop them now and again! Why? I guess it's down to a lack of time, everyday stresses of work and everything else … and a bit of exhaustion!

**Anything else you'd like to share to help towards an imperfectly natural world?** Just a whole lot of idealism about how the world should really be… but I could go on for hours!

based upon anecdotal evidence but toddlers in cloth nappies appear to be toilet trained earlier. It's undoubtedly because they are more aware of feeling wet or uncomfortable, as the moisture is not whisked away as quickly as it is in a disposable. Cloth is also more reliable, they shouldn't leak and a well-fitting nappy will contain a baby's poo better than a disposable. Cloth is more comfortable and many cloth users with older babies or toddlers will tell you that their children prefer cloth nappies to the feel of a disposable.

Cloth is also cute! Cloth nappies are soft, snug and look adorable. The unfortunate consequence of this is that addiction to cloth nappies is not unheard of and can result in your credit card taking a bit of a hit. Now you really do think I'm barking, don't you? I'd never heard myself saying 'I love nappies' until I kitted my third out in his lovely organic cotton, shaped nappy with leopard skin print wrap! The Cornish Real Nappy Project has a guide to the different types of cloth nappy (visit **www.crnp.org.uk**).

## All-in-one nappies

For their convenience and user-friend-liness, all-in-ones are my favourites. You don't need to worry about folding or separate covers as these have their waterproof cover attached to the absorbent layer and a choice of either poppers or Velcro to fasten them.

## Shaped nappies

Again, forget folding, these are shaped to fit baby and most fasten with either Velcro or poppers. You will need a separate waterproof cover but they dry faster than all-in-one nappies.

## Flat nappies

These dry quickly, they are cheaper than most other nappy types and you will need to use a waterproof cover (wrap) over the top,

## Terry squares

Just like the ones mum and dad used and they are still incredibly popular. Don't be afraid of the origami – it was very simple once somebody showed me how. You can forget pins too; parents in the know now use 'nappi nippas' which grip the terry and hold the nappy securely without spiking the baby.

## Prefolds

Rectangular nappies that fold into a pad with the thickest section usually in the middle. They slot into a selection of covers without the use of a separate fastening.

All the nappies use liners and these can be washable or disposable. I found that the paper liners screwed up a bit on the baby, a bit like a wad of toilet paper in your knickers but they were good at catching much of the poo and you can flush them down the loo. The fleece liner is excellent and you can kind of 'sluice' it as you flush the loo before chucking it into the bucket with the soiled nappy.

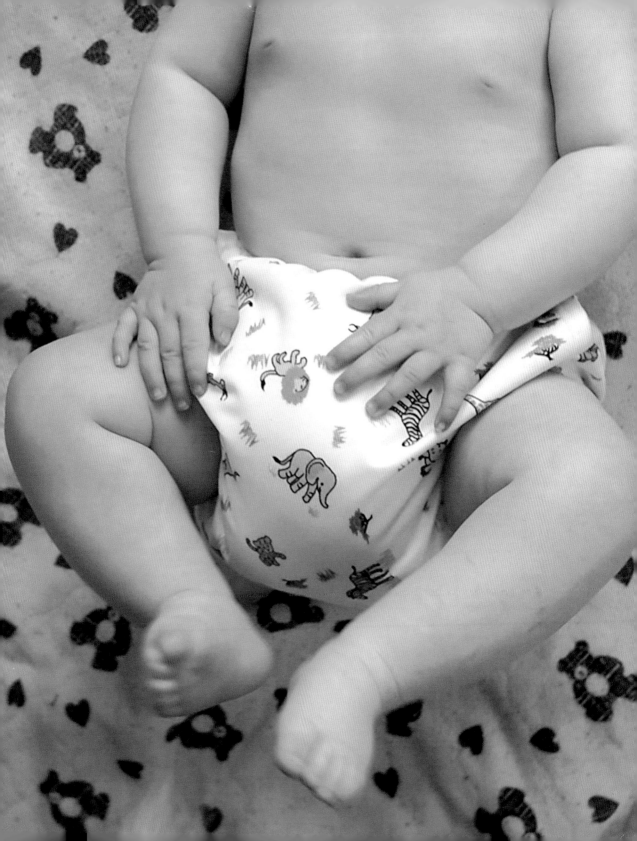

# A word about the laundry

I dreaded doing three extra loads of laundry every day when it already seemed like there was a regular mountain generated by mucky little boys, but it was really no hassle at all. The first myth is that nappies have to be boiled or washed separately at a high temperature. Not so. For starters, there are coloured nappies and they're made from a huge range of fabrics from organic cotton to fleece (which dries very quickly). They can be chucked in with the regular wash at thirty or forty degrees. As for the energy consumption, the truth is, everyone uses their washing machine more frequently once there's a new baby and nappies don't significantly increase that usage.

Cloth nappies wash beautifully with eco-friendly laundry detergents. Don't use fabric conditioner because it will affect their absorbency. Even better than detergents are balls and nuts

– yes, I'm proud to have introduced the nation to laundry balls and soapnuts. Both are kind to the environment and your skin, and they help to retain brightness and colour.

Laundry balls are supercharged with ionised pellets that change the molecular structure of the water. They ionise it and draw the dirt and grime away from the clothes and linens (see **www.aquaball. com**).

Soapnuts are little wonders of nature and have been used for thousands of years in India and Nepal; they're an entirely renewable resource. When the shells come into contact with water, they release saponin (soap) – which washes your laundry without the need for any chemicals. Just put six to eight shells into a little linen drawstring bag and pop them in the drum of the machine. You can re-use them for between three and six washes. Most people use them until they look really brown and knackered and have almost disintegrated, then put them on the compost. Visit **www.ethics trading.com** or **www.soapods.com**.

If you want to mix whites with coloured items you can use a sheet of Colour Catcher, the ingenious blotting paper that goes at the back of the machine and stops your white nappies from turning pink when you've accidentally put in a red

T-shirt. It's available from **www.colour catcher.co.uk** and in supermarkets.

If you're a fan of tumble drying, you'll find that it makes cloth nappies come up beautifully fluffy but it would be remiss of me to recommend hours of expensive reverse-action, not very green, tumbling. Get yourself an old-fashioned spin dryer, which will get rid of all the excess moisture in two minutes instead.

Another concern that I had was the dreaded buckets of stinky nappies. Well, I needn't have worried there either. You can get nappy buckets or any decent-size buckets with a well-fitting lid from just about anywhere and, once the lid is on and you've added some essential oil, there's no unpleasant smell at all. In fact, I think it's far preferable to the whiff of the rubbish sack full of pooey disposables.

You can also forget soaking your dirty nappies in water or expensive solutions. The trendy expression is 'dry-pailing'. Once you've flushed the nappy liner and/or its contents down the loo, stick the nappy in a bucket with a couple of drops of tea tree oil and put the lid on. A bucket of nappies can wait until you do the next load of washing. If you simply must soak, then use bicarbonate of soda and tea tree oil in the water to keep it fresh. If you have left it a few days before washing you'll find it's the water that stinks when it goes stagnant, rather than the nappy.

## Going cloth

If you are interested in 'going cloth', there are organisations out there that are dedicated to converting you to the wonderful world of washable nappies. They offer advice on the phone, will visit and send you free stuff to try out.

Even people at the local council can help, as they are concerned about environmental issues. Try **www.nappyalliance.com** and **www.teamlollipop.co.uk** for lots more information and advice.

For more on the environmental impact of real nappies, go to Women's Environmental Network at **www.wen. org.uk**.

Some of the many excellent companies that make and sell nappies and all things nappy-related include:

www.twinkleontheweb.co.uk
www.babyarmadillo.com
www.underthegooseberrybush.co.uk
www.freerangekids.co.uk
www.treehuggermums.co.uk

RECOMMENDED ECO-FRIENDLY
NATURAL COMMERCIAL PRODUCTS

**ECOVER** The one big 'green' company that manages to jostle alongside the Procter & Gambles and Unilevers of this world in the supermarkets.

**BIO D www.biodegradable.biz**

**SONNET www.greenfibres.com**

**NATURAL CLEAN** make an excellent Orange Degreaser and Multi-Purpose Cleaner **www.naturalclean.co.uk**

**NATURAL HOUSE** make a great cleaner for glass and mirrors called Window Spa. **www.natural-house.com**

**HOME SCENTS** offer a whole range of cleaning stuff including a fantastic Nursery Cleaner (an all-natural spray for cleaning high chairs and potties etc.) and a scented ironing water **www.homescents.co.uk** or **www.baby scents.co.uk**

# Green clean

'Cleaning your house while your kids are still growing is like shovelling the walk [drive] before it stops snowing.'
PHYLLIS DILLER

Having talked about laundry, we should touch on general cleaning. Potentially toxic chemicals are all around us and our homes and most household cleaning products, and for that matter paints, contain VCOs – volatile organic compounds (sounds like an angry carrot pie, doesn't it?). Sadly, these compounds evaporate easily and build up in the air, and can aggravate children prone to asthma.

Many synthetic chemical cleaners are petroleum-based, and many washing detergents contain phosphates to improve their cleaning power – but not your baby's sensitive skin. Many cleaning products contain 'parfum' (artificial fragrances) and are manufactured from petrochemicals. It may freak you out to know that many of these are classed as 'hazardous waste'.

The accumulative effects of household cleaning products may give us headaches, increased symptoms of asthma and hyperactivity, but what do they do to the environment? Because let's face it, we should care about that too, now that we've contributed to the population of further generations. Most commercial cleaning products don't easily biodegrade; they take ages, possibly years, to break down.

So, what are the alternatives? Thankfully there are lots, from companies using kinder plant-based chemicals, to travelling back fifty years and getting out the lemon juice, vinegar and using a large dollop of elbow grease.

## Cleaning

To do your cleaning old-style, all you need is some white vinegar and newspaper (for cleaning the windows), bicarbonate of soda, lemons and some essential oils. To clean most surfaces, I fill a bowl with hot water and a cupful of bicarb and I use an 'e-cloth'(**www.e-cloth.co.uk**). You can also buy great mits and cloths from **www.enjo.co.uk**.

I use a few drops of tea tree oil when cleaning as it is antibacterial. For the loo, I use distilled white vinegar and borax. Replace your loo brush regularly! Remember: nothing makes sinks, baths and loos sparkle like lemon juice!

By the way, for all-purpose cleaning, steam cleaners are a great investment.

## Smell-busting

It's easy to rid the home of smells naturally (there'll be a few with a baby in tow). The answer is bicarbonate of soda. Among its many uses, it's entirely brilliant for soaking up most smells. Just leave a little open box of bicarb in a room and it will soak up any odours. You can also use it in place of commercial vacuum powders. To bulk-buy, try **www.dri-pak.co.uk**.

As for freshening the air, fill a plant spray with water and a couple of drops of essential oil and that's it! If you like a fresh 'antiseptic' kind of whiff, use tea tree oil. Leave a cut of lemon out too for a zingy whiff.

# Baby skin

'Even when freshly washed and relieved of all obvious confections, children tend to be sticky.'

FRAN LEBOWITZ

## Cleaning your baby's bottom

Initially cotton wool and water is all you'll need to clean the folds of skin around your baby's bum (remember, gently wipe down for a girl, up for a boy). As for disposable baby wipes, my top tip is to avoid them. They contain a cocktail of synthetic chemicals that, interestingly, can shift felt-tip pen marks and ink that nothing else can shift! I'm imperfect so I do still use baby wipes but only the organic, chemical-free ones such as Ellie Smellie Baby wipes from **www.spirit ofnature.co.uk** and Tendercare chemical-free flushable wipes from **www.natural child.co.uk** and the

biodegradable ones from **www.earth-friendly-baby.co.uk**.

The better option is to buy washable wipes or cut up pieces of absorbent material and when you're done, stick them in the nappy bucket. For cleanser and moisturer, use two chamomile tea bags, almond or olive oil and a drop of essential oil (lavender is great and soothing for baby skin) added to two mugs of hot water. You can put this into a spritzer bottle once it's cooled, or you can pour the mixture over your wipes in a plastic container. You can come up with lots of your own combinations, though it's best to wait until your baby's six weeks old before introducing essential oils.

You can carry an 'out and about' cleansing spray with you. Half fill an atomiser with water and a few drops of essential oil such as eucalyptus, lavender or tea tree. Spritz a tiny bit in any stinky bags and use it to clean the baby-changing mat and even the skin. It will be antibacterial and antifungal but, if you're not using a preservative, you'll need to change the water regularly. Keep it upright in your changing bag too unless you can find an atomiser with a snap-on lid.

## Looking after the cord

You'll be advised on looking after the cord by the midwives. Just be sure to pull back the nappy so that it doesn't irritate and sponge around the area with a pad of cotton wool soaked in warm water. Don't be tempted to put anything antiseptic on it as nature will encourage it to heal and hopefully fall away quite quickly.

## Cleaning your baby's skin

Never, in my humble opinion, have we been sold a pup like the commercial babycare product. The advertising is always great and the baby washes, creams, oils et al are all, allegedly, 'gentle', 'soft' and 'kind' to your baby's delicate skin. I beg to differ. Some contain a scary cocktail of synthetic chemicals that are, at best, unnecessary and, at worst, potentially hazardous. Here's a quick rundown of some of the ingredients you may want to avoid:

PARABENS (look for methyl, propyl, butyl, ethyl) – preservatives that inhibit microbial growth and can cause skin rashes and allergic reactions.

SODIUM LAURYL SULPHATE (SLS) – a detergent used for its foam-building abilities. Can cause eye irritation and, when combined with other ingredients, it can form nitrosamines which can potentially cause cancer.

TRIETHANOLAMINE (TEA) – another detergent used in baby shampoos to prevent eye sting. Paradoxially, this can cause allergic problems to eyes in some cases! In combination with other ingredients, it is

strongly linked to the promotion of cancer. The list goes on: propylene glycol, PVP/VA copolymer, stearalkonium chloride, synthetic colours, synthetic fragrances. Before I start sounding like a text book, you get the general picture. All are allegedly safe but I say steer clear.

Tiny babies don't, in fact, need to be washed in anything other than water, at least for the first month. Their skin is thinner, more absorbent and more susceptible to harsh chemicals than ours. They just don't need soaps, shower gels, moisturisers or shampoos. And as for talc, you don't even want to know what most brands contain!

Babies also don't need to be given a bath daily. As long as they're topped and tailed then a bath every few days is quite enough. When you do bathe them, although I'm very anti most baby kit, I did find Lulu loved the 'tummy tub'; they call it the 'womb with a view'! This enables babies to adopt to the foetal position and feel calm (**www.tummytub.co.uk**).

## Water

Since I've now hopefully got you just using water, the quality of the water is important. It's amazing how much skin irritation arises from the drying effects of chlorine. Bathing babies in chlorinated tap water can rob skin and hair of their natural protective oils, sometimes causing scaling

and itching. Chlorine also kills much of the beneficial bacteria on the surface of the skin that create a natural defence against skin disorders.

Enter the Dechlorination Crystal Ball. This is not some bizarre unit for clairvoyants, but a filter that basically removes 99.7 per cent of chlorine from the bath water as you run the tap. When I first got mine I was sceptical about whether it would work but I used it and, while I didn't feel as though I was Cleopatra bathing in milk, I couldn't smell chlorine – but then, I couldn't remember smelling it before either. The next evening DH ran a bath for me and I asked him to remember to run the water through the ball. I got into the bath and the smell of chlorine hit me and the water felt really hard. I was convinced that the ball didn't work until I realised that it was in fact completely dry and still sitting on the shelf.

It's perfect and totally safe for a baby's tender skin and for anyone with eczema or a chlorine sensitivity (see **www.the naturalcollection.com**).

## Baby soaps

When you do need to use a few soaps, there are some nice products around that avoid the nasties. I like the Sensitive Skincare Company's All Natural Baby Cleansing Gel, a foaming body wash with organic lavender essential oil (visit www.sensitiveskincareco.com). It's organic and Soil Association-accredited.

For washing hair, the organic baby shampoo from Green People is very mild and available in good health food shops. You can get a natural 'starter set' from www.lavera.co.uk and there's a whole natural range of shampoos, washes and even bubble bath from www.earth-friendly-baby.co.uk. Other very natural companies include www.purenuffstuff.co.uk and www.absolutelypure.co.uk.

## Towels

See page 65 for more on the scary 'ingredients' of many fabrics. If you can afford it, buy gorgeous organic towels from www.organictowel.co.uk and linens from www.peopletree.co.uk.

## Nappy rash

It's highly likely that there'll come a time when, whatever nappy you use, your baby will get nappy rash. And it probably won't creep up on you; it will be more a case of one minute, soft silky skin, the next red, raw and blotchy. Sometimes the rash originates from within and can be attributed to too many processed and refined foods either in the baby's or the mother's diet but often it's caused by the fact that the whole area is a heat and moisture trap.

The excellent news is that I have the answer.

It's seen me through four itchy bottoms and a good many outbreaks of eczema and irritated skin. It's yet another product from the Sensitive Skincare Company, called All Natural Baby Essential Pre-Wash and Massage Oil. You only need apply a fine film around the area and massage it in gently and, trust me, it works like a miracle with only one or two applications. It's a blend of anti-inflammatory and anti-bacterial pure plant oils and it can also be used for massaging dry skin and as a barrier oil.

There's also an excellent nappy rash cream at www.purepotions.co.uk. As a simple moisturiser, pure virgin coconut oil works well. Coconoil is a good one: www.coconoil.com. If you want effective nappy rash cream to make yourself, mix equal parts of zinc and castor oil with one drop of yarrow and one drop of lavender. It's a wonderful cream for any skin irritation and particularly good for chicken pox.

Also let your baby go nappiless occasionally. Just getting fresh air to the area will help.

## Eczema

This can be horrendous for young babies. Don't get it confused with the spots and little rashes that many babies get for the first three weeks or so. Often this is just their hormones kicking in after birth. Minor rashes and skin irritations shouldn't cause concern because they can be the body's way of eliminating toxins but for

'One of the
most important
things you can
give your baby
is a cuddle'

some, outright eczema that obviously itches until it hurts is very distressing.

There's no doubt there has been a rise in allergies and eczema in babies and it's often due to a combination of factors. If your baby has pimples, rashes or very itchy dry skin then it's usually an indication of something going on internally, rather than just on the surface. You'll need to see a nutritionist or allergy-testing specialist if it continues. Often the problem is a milk intolerance that needs to be addressed from within which is not easy when the poor baby is only on milk. If the baby is formula-fed, consider changing to a goat's milk formula that can be less allergenic. If the baby is eating solids, look carefully at the ingredients, particularly if the foods contain flavourings and colourings.

Reactions to wheat and dairy are very common. Remember that your own diet, medication or supplements play a part if you are breastfeeding. Also, take a good look at the external irritants that are coming into contact with your baby's skin, whether directly from skin products or indirectly from the fabric of clothing to the detergents or fabric softener used in the laundry (see page 65 on organic cotton).

With regard to creams and treatments, I would avoid over-the-counter options and definitely any kind of steroid treatment. A healing calendula cream will work a treat on eczema. You can get ready-made massage oil blends and hydrosols from www.sensitiveskin careco.com and their Instant Relief is exactly that – a quick, natural, gentle spray that is safe for babies and children and gives instant relief from any rashes.

## Cradle cap

I've always just left well alone and it seems to rub off of its own accord, but if you think it may be uncomfortable, rub it gently with olive oil. Pure virgin coconut oil is also good for cradle cap and as an all-round moisturiser.

## General skin irritations

For skin irritations or itchiness from bites, always keep the homeopathic remedy Apis in your natural first aid cupboard. The first time we went camping, much to my little boys' delight, I got a huge mosquito bite on my bum! It itched tremendously and the next night I was bitten again. Immediately, I took a pilule of Apis and the itching stopped at once. When little Buddy was bitten, he did the same and, lo and behold, no itching (see page 139 for more on a natural medicine cabinet).

For itching and irritated skin, whatever the cause, even if it's from chicken pox, you'll find great relief from a couple of very simple and fairly old-fashioned remedies.

## Chamomile tea bath

Just steep three chamomile teabags in about a pint of boiling water or use fresh chamomile tea. Strain it and add to a small amount of cool bath water. Let the baby or child sit in the water and find a duck or similar bath toy to amuse him for about ten minutes.(By the way, this is also meant to be a fantastic remedy for piles should you be unlucky enough to get them in pregnancy!)

## Oatmeal bath

This is wonderfully soothing for babies and children. Take a linen bag, an old stocking or a tied up muslin square. Put a cup of rolled porridge oats into the bag and pour the water through it into the bath. Then use the filled bag to wash the child instead of a flannel or soap. It feels a bit like bathing in milk, and is brilliant for itchy skin. For once, it doesn't have to be organic oats!

## Sunscreen

The important thing is to cover up. I know it's a devil to keep a hat on a baby over about six months but do your best. For excellent protective clothing, go to www.suntogs.co.uk. For the exposed bits and for swimming you'll need sunblock but what you absolutely don't need is the regular stuff that's laden with potentially toxic chemicals that can be far more damaging than the sun. I use the organic baby and children sunblock from www.greenpeople.co.uk. There's also a great synthetic, chemical-free zinc oxide sunblock that doesn't give you a white nose from Caribbean Blue (visit www.olive organic.co.uk). For sunburn, see Imperfectly Naturally . . . Unwell (page 138).

Watch what you use on your own skin too because you're in very close contact with your baby and most of what is on you will be affecting him.

## Baby massage

The importance of touch for newborn babies cannot be overestimated and one of the most important things you can give your baby is a cuddle. We all know it can cure the worst of scrapes and bumps, and touch therapy for all ages, especially for babies, is an excellent healer. You may have heard of premature babies who, when stroked or massaged several times a day, begin to thrive and come out of intensive care much sooner than expected.

Massage is relaxing, it brings emotional pleasure, can help with mild pain, stimulate the skin to eliminate toxins and even give a boost to the immune system. These days, many parents want to know how to massage their baby properly and, if you can't make it to an organised class, the good news is, it's very simple.

Choose a time in the day when you can relax and connect with your baby. As he

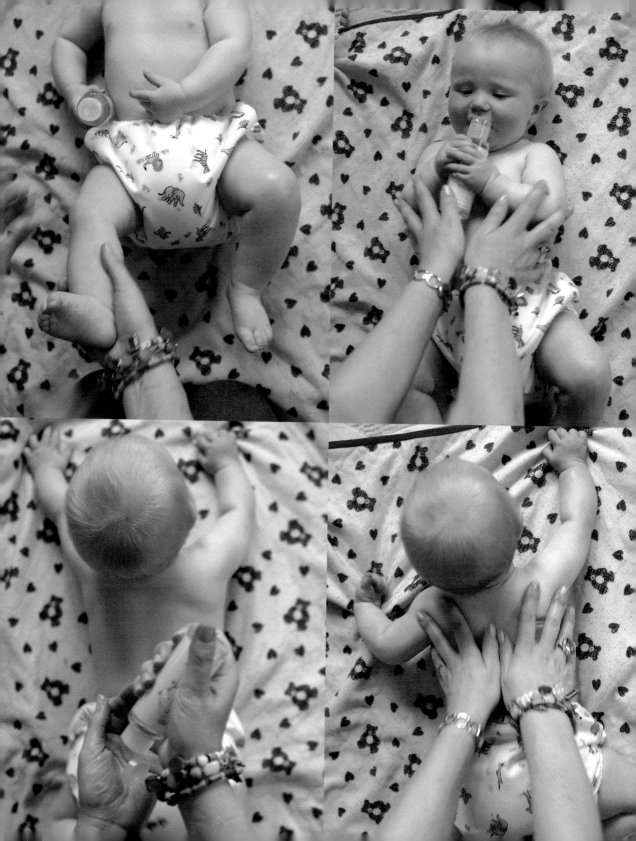

gets a little bit older, a relaxing massage just before bedtime will often send him off to sleep but initially, choose a time when your baby is quite alert and can really benefit from the experience.

One great tip is to wear essential oils occasionally. In this way, the baby becomes accustomed to the aroma from an early age. Lavender, vanilla or rose otto are all good scents. You could put one drop on a tissue and keep it tucked into your bra or use a Wrist Angel, a bracelet impregnated with essential oils (**www.wrist angel.co.uk**).

There are lots of base oils that you can use for baby massage. My favourites are coconut oil (see page 57) and sweet almond, but even regular olive oil is good.

If you want to use essential oils, it's a good idea to do a sensitivity test first. Mix up the oil with a base oil and apply a tiny bit to a patch of skin. Wait at least an hour then, if there's no adverse reaction, go ahead. Just be aware that essential oils can be dangerous and, of course, if you're pregnant you'll need to be very aware of contra-indications and, whatever happens, never use lavender oil on yourself or massage others with it. On another safety note, remember always to keep your oils in a dark cool place out of reach of children. For a massage on babies aged up to eighteen months, use only a couple of drops of essential oil in 20 ml of carrier oil (use a base oil such as jojoba, olive oil, almond oil).

Some very relaxing essential oils to add to the base include: lavender (antiseptic, calming and good for clearing nostrils), chamomile roman (good for inducing sleep and calming digestion), myrhh (good for encouraging the elimination of mucus, so great for newborns).

If you're at all concerned about mixing your own essential oils, try one of the ready-made oils specially formulated for babies. You can choose from an excellent range of organic essential oils at **www. essentiallyoils.com** and from **www.eoco. org.uk** where a range of candles, chill pillows and even magnatherapy bracelets are also available.

An excellent book is **Aromatherapy and Massage for Mother and Baby: How Essential Oils Can Help You in Pregnancy and Early Motherhood** by Allison England (Vermilion).

# Teeth

It's sometimes only a matter of months before you see the first signs of teeth in babies. From the moment they appear, they're going to need cleaning. If you're breastfeeding exclusively for the first five or six months, breast milk luckily does not have an adverse effect on teeth, so you don't need to go mad with a baby toothbrush. However, it's good to get them into the routine and the feeling of having their teeth cleaned, initially just with water. You can't be too laid back on this just because they're milk teeth; they still need them for a few years to come, especially as the embryonic adult teeth actually exist in a soft, uncalcified state below them and they can be put in danger if decay or infection reaches the roots of the milk teeth.

So, what to use? It won't surprise you if I go a bit old style again, will it? Most regular toothpastes are full of, in my humble opinion, unnecessary nonsense including artificial sweeteners, flavourings and, of course, fluoride.

## The fluoride debate

For me, the issue is simple: not only does fluoride make a great rat poison, it's a drug and it's toxic to humans. The idea that a government can have the power to infiltrate a dangerous drug into millions of people via, what should be, their pure and natural water supply is borderline science fiction. But that's exactly what's been happening in the name of public health, for the last forty years. Even some pro-fluoridation scientists argue that levels may now already be too high as the population is already receiving high doses from toothpaste alone. Our teeth may have less fillings but at what cost? Fluoride

affects bone density and, even more worrying is its neurotoxic effect on developing brain function, motor function and learning ability. Other scientists will argue that the doses are small but, again, we've heard it all before. It's the cumulative effect that I'm always banging on about. It's another toxin being absorbed into our system, along with the thousand other small doses, combining to create a lethal cocktail.

Rant over, other than to say 'no thanks'! I remove it from water before I drink it by means of a reverse-osmosis under-sink filter and I always look for non-fluoride and natural toothpastes. I would prefer to reduce the possibility of fillings in my kids by a different approach to diet and eating habits.

## Toothpastes

For the kids, it's hard to beat Organic Children's Toothpaste from Green People at **www.greenpeople.co.uk**. My toddler really seems to like the mandarin variety but, generally, they will get used to the taste of any of the good adult varieties that the whole family can use.

Try the Kingfisher range (from most health shops) and the lemon toothpaste from Miessence organics **www.mionegroup. com** and the strawberry children's one from **www.lavera.co.uk**. Toddlers will swallow the toothpaste rather than spit it out so in a

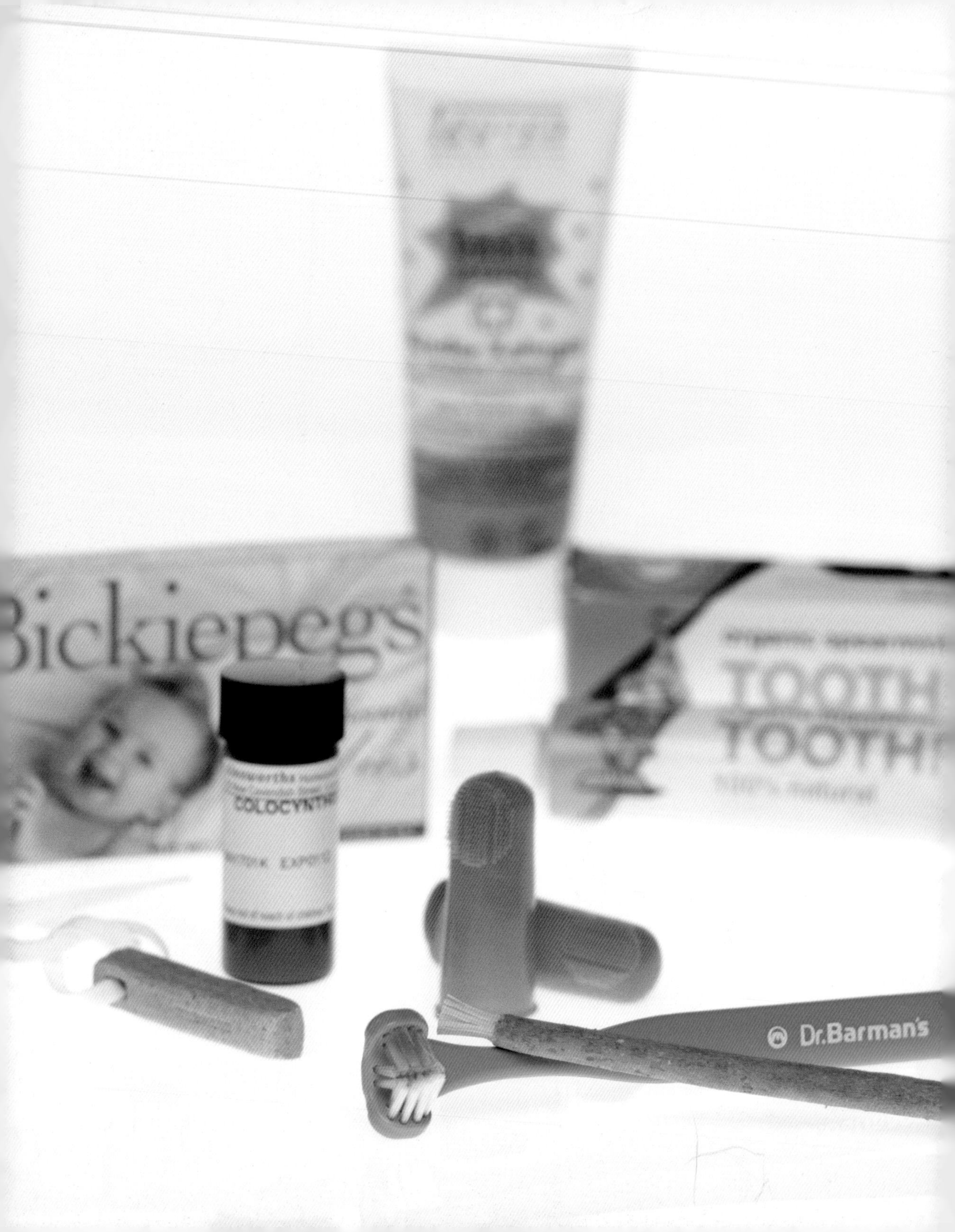
Bickiepegs
TOOTH
TOOTH
Dr.Barman's

way, I prefer that it's not too tasty. It's also another good reason for using only toothpastes with high-quality natural ingredients. It's easy to make your own toothpaste; the only tricky bit is retraining your taste buds. Try bicarbonate of soda, which acts as a mild abrasive, and water but, here's a nice tip, just add one drop of peppermint oil.

## Brushes

When it comes to brushes, most are too big for tiny mouths and quite difficult for you to manoeuvre 'upstairs and downstairs' to reach their little gums. Enter The Finger Toothbrush, a tiny little 'finger' with gentle rubber bristles that you wear on your own finger to enable you gently to clean your baby's teeth and gums. It's a brilliant innovation. The company that make them are Bickiepegs who make the teething biscuits. They also go on to the next stage with the Superbrush, a toothbrush with all-round bristles for toddlers. You can buy them online at **www.bickie pegs.co.uk**.

For you, by the way, there's also The Natural Toothbrush. It's taken from the root of the Araak tree; it looks like

a twig and it's perfect for travelling. It's available in health shops and pharmacies (or visit **www.naturaltoothbrush.com**).

# Baby clothing and bags

## Organic cotton

We check the ingredients in food, skincare and cleaning products but what about our clothes? Well, did you know that eleven per cent of all the world's pesticides are used on cotton, with most of it ending up in the environment and the food chain or on your baby's delicate skin. Thousands of synthetic chemicals are used in its production and

nearly half of all cotton made in the USA is genetically modified (GM). So I would say, go organic if you can. With four children, my 'greenness' stands proud when it comes to their clothing; I reuse and recycle. All my kids wear hand-me-downs and when I buy new, it's organic.

So, what do organic cotton garments look like? Stylish and funky! It won't surprise you to know that I don't buy designer clothes for my kids. I can't get my head around spending a fortune on cashmere babygrows that last eight weeks. Anyway, because organic and fairly traded items are not usually mass-produced, they're individual and almost designer. You don't see many others wearing the same top. Lots of companies now do ethically traded organic kit, some even made from bamboo fibre.

## Recycle

I'll never say no to a bag of old clothes from a mum whose kids have grown. The trick is to make sure you know someone who has slightly older children than yourself. It saves you a fortune and you can do the same for someone else later.

I love finding unusual clothes and I'm the Queen of Charity Shop Chic. Most items probably won't be organic or ethical but at least they're being recycled and are affordable, and the money's going to a good cause. Why not have a rummage yourself. Most charity shops have a fast turnover of great clothes for kids.

Once your children are old enough, they can choose their own outfits. Mind you, we once popped out for a walk with Rocky when he was two and forgot to check his clothes. He'd chosen a long T-shirt decorated with felt pen, some Union Jack wellies and nothing else! It was wonderful to see the smiles on the faces of the passers-by.

## Clothes for cloth nappies

Babies in cloth nappies look so cute with their padded bottoms but finding clothes to fit over their rear can be a problem. Enter Cut4cloth (**www.cut4cloth.co.uk**). This company makes high-quality, funky and gorgeous, one hundred per cent organic, ethically manufactured and reasonably priced clothing, which is usually longer and wider to allow freedom of movement with a bigger bum! I've got a lovely babygrow that says '100% Organic Baby' on the front and a T-shirt with the words 'Eco-ungel'. If you don't use real nappies you can still buy their stuff. Check the sizing, they are generous. See also **www.greenbaby.co.uk**, **www.tatty bumpkin.com** and **www.eco-eco.co.uk**.

## Shoes

One of the cutest items you'll ever see is your baby's first bootees, though they're

Pesticides Action Network UK (combating the environmental effects of pesticides) **www.pan-uk.org** and Labour Behind the Label (raising awareness of working conditions in the garment industry) **www.labour behind thelabel.org**.

## Bags

I must admit I am a bit of a bag lady and having a new baby was a great excuse to add to the collection. There is a fantasic selection of baby kit bags to choose from but I found the best to be a regular waterproof mini rucksack with a few zipped compartments. Always get good-quality ones as the zips break on cheaper ones and make sure they are from ethical companies. Most cheaper ones, besides not being fairly traded, are coated in horrible chemicals. I once bought a cheap suitcase from a high street store. I removed the plastic covering at home and almost keeled over from the whiff of formaldehyde!

Much has been documented on the plastic shopping bag mountain but there are now supermarket initiatives with 'bags for life' and many eco-friendly alternatives. There are lovely organic cotton, hessian bags. Remember the old 1970s string bags, so tiny you could pop them in your pocket? I particularly like Turtle Bags, available from **www.turtlebags.co.uk**. The name refers to the fact that many turtles are killed by plastic bags. Leatherbacks travel to the UK

a devil to keep as a pair as they constantly fall off. Shoes are one thing even I don't hand down, mainly because the shape of a baby's foot determines the shape of the shoe.

There are some lovely, undyed, hand-knitted alpaca bootees available from Greenfibres (**www.greenfibres.co.uk**), and Starchild has a fantastic range of leather shoes with lots of designs for kids up to the age of three. They mould to the foot and are coloured with eco-friendly, non-toxic dyes, which are ideal as babies love sucking their toes (**www.star-child.co.uk**).

For further information on organic and fair trade clothing, contact the Soil Association (organic food and farming and sustainable forestry) **www.soilassociation.org**, waters for jellyfish and mistake upturned bags for food. The bags are reusable, fair trade and made from organic jute, sisal or natural cotton. Too many plastic bags find their way into marine animals, so say 'NO' to plastic bags. Many countries have already banned them.

Another innovative design comes from Earthpak (**www.earthpak.com**), a forward-thinking, eco-friendly company. Their high-quality backpacks are made from ninety-eight per cent recycled plastic bottles. The average Earthpak saves over twelve two-litre bottles from landfill. They're shredded, processed into a fibre, spun into yarn, woven into a durable fabric and dyed in an environmentally friendly manner. There's a great range of colours including girlie pink. Check out their Enviro-Bebe changing-bag range. They say it's a diaper bag, backpack and changing station all in one. See Earthpak's range and other excellent recycled bags at **www.thenatural collection.com**.

# Baby-wearing and swaddling

## Baby-wearing

Attachment parenting is often linked to baby-wearing. This is an age-old concept with a trendy name. In other cultures, for generations, women have carried babies either on their back or their front in wraparound slings so they can go about their daily business. Once I'd found the right sling for me, a Kari-me Wraparound (**www.kari-me.co.uk**), I loved carrying my baby for long periods at a time. Life actually got easier as I could breastfeed while on the phone, cook, work, walk around the supermarket and play with my toddler. Venturing out, there were none of the problems associated with buggies and stairs. I even found myself socialising and reading the newspaper while downing cappuccinos as if I were on my own.

The baby was content nearly all the time, rarely cried and seemed very happy with all the motion as I went about my everyday activities. Sleep was comfortable and undisturbed by my continual movement and she actually slept better in the sling than anywhere else. It's a fantastic bonding experience and I would absolutely recommend carrying your baby as much as you can.

There are lots of slings available, including wraparounds, ring slings, pouch slings and soft carriers, as well as backpacks. Your choice is a personal thing. Firstof all, the sling must be comfortable; anything that hangs from your shoulders, especially with thin straps, is going to strain after a while. The weight needs to be evenly distributed, so look for a sling that takes the weight around the back and torso, while keeping baby as close to your body as possible.

I started off with a front-pack, papoose-style sling (Baby Bjorn) but quickly realised that, for me, it wasn't great for newborns and I really needed a sling in which I could easily breastfeed the baby. I progressed to a ring sling, then found the wonder of the wraparound. Have a good look at the options and remember, you can always buy them second-hand to try them out. Fortunately, they are not nearly as expensive as buggies, so you can afford more than one if you want a different variety for a toddler.

Once you get into slings, they do become a bit addictive, rather like cloth nappies, as they are very fashionable and come in a huge range of colours and patterns. Let's face it, you'll need at least two to go with different outfits! Some women, who really are heading for a halo, make their own; indeed, that's how many work-at-home mums start their own businesses. They make so many slings that it becomes a little industry.

Laura Park, who runs Brightspark Slings (**www.brightsparkslings.co.uk**), says: 'The business was never really meant to be a business. In 2002 I had a baby, Alexander, and he just refused to be put down. He cried for about twelve hours a day and became hysterical if he was left for a minute! I made a sling after finding my high street carrier extremely uncomfortable and Alexander was immediately much calmer. A friend asked me to make one for her baby, then another friend asked and another. Soon I was making twenty slings a week and realised that this could be the ideal way of staying at home with my baby, which was very important to me, while doing something "for me". I had been diagnosed with post-natal depression and it gave me a great boost to help other people with babies who were unsettled and I am sure it helped my recovery.'

If you get into all of this big-time, you can meet lots of like-minded baby-wearers on dedicated websites and forums such as **www.slingmeet.co.uk**. You can get great slings too from **www.little possums. co.uk**, **www.babyarmadillo. co.uk** and **www.thecarryingkind.co.uk**.

## Swaddling

It's an old-fashioned word and one that's usually associated with Christmas carols, but swaddling is making something of a comeback. An age-old practice that's long been out of fashion in Britain, it's remained common practice in many other cultures. It seems to have made its name as an effective way of getting babies off to sleep quickly and it's certainly a fact that newborn babies like to feel secure. They've been curled up in a very tight space in the womb and one of the first times you'll hear a really loud cry from your baby is as they emerge into the bright cruel world as their arms and legs are drawn away from their usual foetal position.

Swaddling does have its critics. Deborah Jackson in her excellent book **Three in a Bed** (Bloomsbury) writes 'Mothers in eighteenth-century Britain bound their babies tightly and hung them out of the way . . . while the half-strangled baby hung from a nail, its minder could get on with other tasks. Swaddling slowed down a baby's heartbeat and encouraged extreme passivity – more sleep, less crying, a swaddled baby made no demands on the adult world around it . . . Societies that practice swaddling have recognised the infant's need for bonding, but they bind the child to itself rather than the mother.'

Leaving babies swaddled is therefore something I wouldn't recommend. If you do swaddle your baby, always use a cellular cotton blanket. I believe that the way to get the best that swaddling can offer it is to 'wear' your baby. A great safe but snug travel wrap is the Baby Hoodie (**www.morrck.com**).

# Sleeping

'There never was a child so lovely but his mother was glad to get him to sleep'
RALPH WALDO EMERSON

Before we get on to the tricky stuff of getting your baby to sleep through the night, let's start with ourselves and look at the industry that's emerged around our nocturnal habits. We have 24-hour radio and television,

24-hour supermarkets and we can talk all night in internet chat rooms. Insomnia is practically a national crisis and doctors regularly prescribe medication to deal with it. In addition to sleeping tablets there is a whole industry of herbal remedies for sleep, special CDs and a massive range of 'sleep-easy' mattresses, pillows and lighting equipment. Who'd have thought something so simple would become such a project?

Then, for us exhausted mothers, there are agencies that now offer night nannies and experts who will help you to establish a good sleep routine for your baby. I actually got to the stage where I rang one of these agencies to discuss the possibility of hiring a night nanny but, although they tried to be helpful, I quickly realised I was too imperfect even for them to be able to help! They claim they can usually sort out sleep problems but I had the tricky situation of a three-week-old baby as well as a two-year-old who was waking four times a night.

You will become obsessed with sleep. The problem can start before you give birth. Pregnancy itself throws up (often literally) some sleep problems. You're more likely to feel agitated or nauseous. During the third trimester you will certainly begin to feel more uncomfortable as your huge bump makes it difficult to stay in one position. You will probably find that you need to wee more often too, so you'll be dragging your huge, sleepy, vertical dolphin shape to the bathroom three or four times a night.

Some people say this happens to help us begin to adjust to the sleepless nights to come but in my honest opinion, it doesn't!

After my baby was born and I was truly in the throes of full-on 24-hour mothering, was I ill and exhausted? Well, there were many times when I was knackered but, the reality is, having a baby brings with it a new kind of energy, although those amazing new resources are not limitless. We still need to find ways to rediscover the natural art of sleep.

## Your bedroom

First of all, let's look at our sleeping environment. I firmly believe that the bedroom should be for sleep and for sex – that's it. You may need to store your clothes in there, but what you absolutely do not want is electrical equipment of any kind buzzing away next to your head. Almost any electrical equipment creates EMFs (electromagnetic fields), which interfere with the brain's sleep pattern.

There are, of course, many other reasons for insomnia, such as psychological factors – stress and depression – and basic dietary issues. But we may also have something to learn from other cultures and societies for whom sleep is not a problem. In her fantastically enlightening book **The Continuum Concept** (Arkana), Jean Liedloff describes a group of South American tribesmen who, despite very real danger from wild animals, are so attuned to sounds that when someone cracks a joke during the night, they all wake, laugh and drop straight back into a sound sleep. If they hear anything that sounds like danger, they wake simultaneously, fully alert.

In **Three in a Bed** (Bloomsbury), Deborah Jackson compares this incredible story with our huge struggle to get enough sleep and wake refreshed, a problem for over two-thirds of adults. She says that many westerners, once disturbed, find it difficult to get back to sleep, which is why babies can wreak such havoc at unholy hours. Deprived, even slightly, of our regular due, we cannot function properly in the day. By

Every time we made an attempt at nookie (quietly), we would glance over to see him wide-eyed and grinning at us – a bit of a passion killer for sure! Eventually we kind of just carried on anyway – he didn't seem to mind.

Imperfectly natural **dad**

the time we are adults, she explains, we are no longer in control of sleep, it controls us.

As a new mum, therefore, you should look after your own sleep issues first. As some life coaches might say, reframe your old beliefs and conditioning about sleep, so you can look at it in a different way and wake up smiling. I do believe effortless sleep is achievable and, in achieving it ourselves, we may be able to prevent transferring some of our own insomnia anxieties to our babies.

Are you consuming foods that interfere with the body's natural patterns? Look at your diet and also consider alcohol, caffeine and additives (see food section, pages 106–37) and don't forget to remove electrical equipment from your bedroom. Look at how you are reacting to stress levels in your day. Remember that stress doesn't come from events; it comes from the way you react to them. All this will affect your sleep. Our babies can sense when, for one reason or another, we're not quite in tune with the natural patterns of life and they will often mirror it. They're trying to tell us something!

## Getting them to sleep

'If your baby is beautiful and perfect, never cries or fusses, sleeps on schedule and burps on demand, an angel all the time, you're the grandma.'

THERESA BLOOMINGDALE

So what is the realistic expectation of the hours a baby should sleep? Of course, there are naps during the day, but it may surprise you to know that a baby is considered to be sleeping through the night if he sleeps for approximately five hours, with the optimum time being between midnight and about 5 a.m. The problem is that if you want to put your baby down to sleep at 7 p.m. to get into some grown-up time, just as you're exhausted and heading off to bed at midnight, your baby is likely to be awake and ready to rock!

One very amusing thing that you'll find happens, however you try to get your baby to sleep, is that when you are almost desperate, they become more adamant that it's not night-time or nap time. I can remember many occasions and still have them now when I've lain down with my baby to try and get her to sleep. Often I've intended to breastfeed her to sleep (I know, it's not advised but it sure does help), or I've been cuddling her and singing softly. After what seems like an age and I'm almost asleep myself, she'll finally drop off. I'll take a peek and, sure enough, she's soundly 'off with fairies'. I then have to try to extricate myself without disturbing her. First things first: remove nipple from mouth, remove arm from behind head or under back, then, somehow, prise self up from mattress without creating huge dip in bed or any noise. Shimmy away from baby. Slither on to knees in low, squatting position from which, slowly and quietly, crawl or tiptoe across floor towards door, avoiding that creaking floorboard. Once at door, look around and smile gratefully that baby is sound asleep. Slowly, open door and slip out, barely breathing. Oh-so-gently close door, making no more sound than a mouse. Breathe out with relief and, just as I reach the stairs, I hear the cry – 'Mummy'! Foiled again!

## A routine?

You will hear conflicting advice as to where your baby should sleep, what time he should go to bed and how long he should sleep. You'll hear experts who tell you that you must never let a baby fall asleep while being cuddled or rocked or – shock horror – while breastfeeding. You'll hear people tell you that it's dangerous to share a bed with your baby and that it's okay for them to 'cry it out' (more on that later). Then there's that annoying word 'routine'.

Everyone will ask if you have your baby's routine established. If you have one that works for you, then good on you and, quite frankly, I'm jealous. I'm not suggesting that a proper routine is a bad thing. It's important, whatever your lifestyle, to encourage a basic one before bedtime and, wherever possible, for naps during the day. I absolutely baulk at listening to the childcare experts who tell us to feed our babies by the clock and put them down for naps at exactly the same time every day. I've even known mothers running late (who doesn't?) to

cancel their appointment because they might arrive at the time the baby needs to nap, which will upset their schedule by fifteen minutes. It means their whole day goes pear-shaped. Relax! With the best will in the world, you can't do this with military precision. This is a baby and day-to-day living, not a factory line or an army camp.

I prefer to use the word 'rhythm' to describe the ideal way to structure the day; 'routine', for me, is too regimental. Of course, babies and young children need a consistent waking time, familiar surroundings and regular meals. The calming down period before bedtime is especially important. I discovered this to my detriment when I, stupidly and imperfectly, expected my two-year-old third, Rocky, just to toddle off to bed at 7 p.m. on a light, hot summer's night while his big brothers were still splashing in the paddling pool. We introduced more of a rhythm to the day, including at least an hour when he would be away from the stimulation of the older boys, have one-to-one attention, bathtime, stories and a quiet play, after which he would be relaxed enough to go off to sleep. For toddlers and older children, after you've read them a story, a gentle story CD will help them drift off (www.relaxkids.com).

## Controlled crying

This issue comes down to two camps. In the one there are those who believe that babies must learn to fall asleep by themselves and, until they learn that important lesson, they must be left to 'cry it out'. The other camp believes that it's quite normal for babies to wake during the night. They think it's the job of the parent to accept that and to nurture and care for them all day and all night, if necessary, until eventually they sleep through the night (when they are ready). Well, it won't surprise you to know that I am certainly not in the 'leave them to cry' camp.

Deborah Jackson makes reference in Three in a Bed to the well-known childcare guru, Dr Benjamin Spock, one of the pioneers of the 'let them cry' method, who managed to convince a whole generation of its alleged benefits. 'The Spock-trained baby has resigned himself to the hopelessness of his situation. He has learnt a cruel lesson that there isn't any point in trying to improve things.' So, why have so many professionals and mothers thought that controlled crying was such a winner? Just plonk him in a cot and let him cry it out? It's so easy – two or three nights of crying for a short time and then he'll sleep through the night. Well, for most people, that's myth. Many parents find that when they try this method, weeks later their baby is still crying for hours and still waking regularly in a hopelessly fretful state. During the day, he is fussy and clingy and often the parent, as well as the baby, is not only exhausted from lack of sleep but also upset by so much crying. If a baby learns

anything at all, it's not to bother trying to communicate when you're distressed. Yet, as we all know, crying is one of the few lines of communication a baby has.

For most women, even those who go along with the controlled crying method, it goes against the grain. I've spoken to many who felt they'd been indoctrinated not to respond to a very basic and natural instinct. The important thing to do, when it comes to sleep issues, as with so much of caring for your new baby, is to use that inbuilt mother's intuition, something that many a so-called professional would have you ignore. A new mum, rather than being a kind of hopelessly uninformed outpatient, released after a nine-month illness, is someone at the height of her natural intuitive powers. Remember, the buck stops with you, not the childcare professional.

## Co-sleeping

Sharing a bed with your baby is yet another old-fashioned, age-old custom that has somehow become taboo in our society. Across the world, parents sleep with their infants and it's seen as entirely normal, healthy and beneficial. The term co-sleeping, or bed-sharing, refers to one or more parents sleeping next to their baby in the same bed.

There have been too many negative things said about co-sleeping. When your child is

'A new mum is someone at the height of her natural intuitive powers'

fractious, fearful or sick and wants to come into your bed, you shouldn't feel guilty. You can join the masses of parents already enjoying this incredible bond with their children that gives them security and huge benefits. However, bed-sharing can be an entirely conscious decision rather than just a response to a middle-of-the-night emergency.

Despite recommendations that it's not a good idea to sleep with a baby under two, polls show that nearly seventy per cent of parents do sleep with their baby for part or all of the night. Before you start yelling at me, 'But there are babies who have been smothered by their parents when they've fallen asleep on the couch!', I will state that, of course, you should not consider co-sleeping unless you have looked fully into the safety issues.

You'll need a very low, firm bed (no water beds!) or preferably a big mattress on the floor with no crevices or gaps where your baby can become wedged, You'll also need to make sure your baby cannot roll off the bed so you may decide to use a side-rail or bedside cot. Don't use pillows before the age of one, and after that, ensure that they are straight and that there are no pillows or blankets that could fall on the infant. Your baby must be able to move freely so should not be swaddled. Never fall asleep with your baby by accident.

Always sleep with safety in mind, the most important point being that no one should be drunk or suffering from the effects of any medication or drugs. Obviously, if you are very overweight, do not have adequate control over your own body, or are a sound sleeper who finds it difficult to wake, co-sleeping won't be for you.

If you're concerned about safety, remember that the cot option is not necessarily safer. We are given umpteen different sets of directions for how to place our babies in their cots and how much safer it is for them to sleep on their backs, but still there are many cot deaths. I remember a talk on natural parenting by renowned paediatrician, Michel Odent, who said that, in many other countries where it is entirely normal for whole families to sleep in one bed, or certainly the same room (usually due to overcrowding, poverty, etc), there is no actual translation for the phenomenon of cot death or Sudden Infant Death Syndrome. They have simply never experienced it. Dr Michel Odent wrote of his findings in The Lancet (25 January 1986): 'I hold the view that, even if it happens during the day, cot death is a disease of babies who spend their nights in an atmosphere of loneliness and that it is a disease of societies where the nuclear family has taken over.' I don't know what the explanation for this is, except perhaps that when your newborn baby is close to you, if there is any change in breathing pattern, body temperature or heart rate, you would sense it and react immediately.

That said, I do feel you must trust your instinct and if the cot option works for you, then that's excellent. Some babies sleep happily alone and night time is never a problem. I just don't want new mothers to feel that it's the only way and I don't want you to miss out on an amazing experience. Being roused by the awful sound of your baby howling in the next room can be a rude awakening but, when babies sleep next to you, they wake up slowly and give a big stretch and a smile.

We found it easier right from the off to have our babies next to us where we knew they were safe. When they're newborn, you listen out for every little breath and, if I'd had to keep running into another room to check my baby was still alive, it would have looked like a West End farce.

I also realised early on that it was much easier to pop a boob into the baby's mouth while I was still lying down and then doze back off to sleep when he'd finished. I wish I had a pound for every time a well-meaning friend, on hearing that we co-slept with our first baby, said: 'You'll make a rod for your own back. Once you start down that route you'll never get him out your bed.' I found the opposite to be true. Our first baby slept with us for about a year and then was very happy to go into his 'big boy's bed' where he slept brilliantly without a peep. I still buy into the theory that if they get their fill of sleeping with their parents,

they tend to be better sleepers later on.

So, how do you make co-sleeping work practically? Well, there are different ways. Some families choose to place their babies in a cot for their daytime naps and for the first few hours of the evening and then just bring them into the family bed if they wake and cry during the night. Others choose not to bother with a cot at all and lay the baby down to sleep on any safe mat or couch in the family room (it's amazing how babies sleep through any noise!), then carry them up to bed when they retire. I have often placed my sleeping baby safely in the middle of my big bed for a few hours and then gone and joined her.

A truly liberating read, however you choose to sleep, is **The No-Cry Sleep Solution** by Elizabeth Pantley, a mother who found controlled crying too cruel and set about devising a gentle series of steps towards a sleep routine. Another great read on this is Tine Thevenin's **The Family Bed** (Avery).

## Sharing the burden

If we lived in communities with extended families, perhaps we would all feel a little more supported by sharing the burden of the night shift, but in our society, it usually comes down to juggling between husband and wife.

Dads and babies have an uncanny knack of being able to sleep together very soundly right through the night, so I can definitely recommend occasionally packing them off to the spare room, spread-eagling yourself over the entire bed and dreaming soundly for a straight eight hours. How imperfect is that? Also, even in their sleep, babies can sense when a ripe boob is nearby, and will wake. It seems that, on the occasional night when it's not there, they don't miss it, so it's definitely worth getting your partner into that one.

## Nurseries

It's bizarre, isn't it, the way you spend a fortune on baby equipment before a baby is born? You kit out a nursery with expensive furniture, a changing table and a super-duper cot with bunny rabbit patterned bedding, only to find that, after day one, no one ventures in there until the child is about two.

Unless your house is like the one in Mary Poppins and you have that fabulous full-time nanny to care for your offspring, you tend to find that your changing area becomes any convenient bit of floor space near the lounge and kitchen. Your baby's clothes and laundry tend to be kept near the nappies by the nappy-changing station or in the washing machine. The babies, when asleep during the day, are either in a car seat, a buggy, or attached to your boob. Of course, there are baby experts who would say babies need a strict routine and should always be placed in their cot to sleep, even if it's only for a nap during the day, but I absolutely don't buy into that.

## Cots and bedding

Nursery furniture can be hideously expensive and parents often go a bit mad on the nursery environment. This is another area where I'd recommend going green, buying second-hand or borrowing where you can, especially the wooden items and decorative stuff. Babies mustn't have pillows initially but when you do want to get one, make it organic if you can.

Most people have a Moses basket or small crib for the first few weeks. You can get one with an organic cotton cover and organic wool rubberised coir (coconut fibre) mattress. These are not cheap but they are high quality; remember though that you'll only use it for the first few weeks. You can also get the Eco-Crib from Mothercare, which is disposable and made of recycled, heavy-duty cardboard. It makes a great 'green' pressie that lasts for a few months.

If you're going to buy a new cot, my advice is to buy a large one that can be extended into a small child's bed by removing the sides. Obviously, you'll need drop-down sides so you can lift the baby in and out without hurting your back. A really good eco-friendly one is the Merlin cot/bed, which is available from **www.greenfibres.co.uk**.

If you buy any second-hand cot or child's bed, always buy a new mattress. In fact, I'd say buy a new mattress even for your subsequent babies. Mattresses are horrors for harbouring bugs, which research has shown could cause infection in babies with weakened immune systems and have even been implicated in cot deaths.

Many people now choose the natural latex, coir-style mattress. Latex is made up of tiny little pores that enable air to circulate freely. It's dust-free and gives protection against bacteria and mould. The latex is enveloped in a thick compacted layer of wool wadding from naturally reared sheep. It's a good idea to choose one with an organic cotton drill outer cover.

As your mattress gets older, spray it and your bedding with Neem anti-mite spray from **www.junglesale.com**.

## Bedside cots

I must say, I did find a bedside cot useful, purely to extend our bed a bit, though I do remember, for the first couple of months, DH seemed to end up curled in it most nights while baby and I stretched out across the mattress! You can get a good 'bed-extending' cot from Mothercare or from **www.tuttibambini.co.uk**.

## Baby hammocks

Sleeping in a hammock is a fantastic way for a baby to get the right sleeping position, with the lovely rocking motion to ease them into a dreamlike state. Much as I wanted to, I couldn't pursue it with Lulu (my fourth) as I knew it would become a fabulous temptation for Rocky to swing her just a fraction too hard into the wall! You can get 100 per cent cotton hammocks that will last up to a year. After that, they can't really take the weight and you'll need a bigger size. Hammocks are available from **www.smilechild.co.uk**, **www.spirit ofnature.co.uk** and **www.handmade hammocks.co.uk** (fair-trade hammocks). It's worth looking for second-hand ones on eBay.

## Sleeping bags

Many mothers prefer a baby sleeping bag to regular bedding sheets or duvets as there's no chance of the baby becoming exposed and, even more important, no danger of the bedding getting caught over the baby's head or around their neck. If possible, get an all-seasons one in 100 per cent organic cotton. I found a fantastic one that has removable sleeves and a removable terry cotton liner for use in spring and summer. It even has special slits that allow the baby to wear it while travelling in a car seat or buggy. It's the Four Seasons sleeping bag from **www.spiritofnature.co.uk**. A nice quality lambskin or fleece is also a worthwhile purchase as is a 'herb pillow' from **www.dreamacres.co.uk**.

'Babies mustn't have
pillows initially, but when
you do want to get one,
make it organic if you can'

# Imperfectly natural parent

**Your name, age group, age of children** Jacinta Jolly, 32, one son aged two, and pregnant again.

**Occupation?** A high-school English teacher. I still like to think of myself as a teacher, just with a much smaller class!

**Birth experiences – natural/assisted?** I had a natural, vaginal birth, assisted by a wonderful midwife and my husband. I had a quick labour and didn't use, or feel I needed, pain relief. I had some labial grazing, and haemorrhaged post-partum, but nothing too serious.

**When did your figure return? Did you exercise?** Pretty quickly, I guess. Aside from a soft belly, I didn't look much like I'd just had a baby, as I didn't put on any weight really. I did exercise, doing a weekly ante-natal workout which was run by the physio department at the hospital where my son was born. I did this for six months after his birth, and felt like I recovered pretty quickly.

**Breastfeeding experience?** I had some soreness for a couple of days post-partum but nothing serious. I am still feeding my two-year-old son. I have qualified as a mother supporter with the Association of Breastfeeding Mothers and work with a peer support group in mid-Wales.

**Nappies – if cloth, which type do your prefer and why?** We have always used cloth nappies. We use cloth squares either inside a 'pocket' nappy, made of PUL and fleece, or covered by a fleece wrap. I have made all of my son's nappy covers, something I was quite obsessed with for a while!

**First foods – home-made purées or jars?** We mostly went for the finger-food option, with some homemade rice congee as well. Mostly it was steamed veggies and a bit of fruit, and eventually some oat porridge. I didn't use jars except in exceptional circumstances – when I was out and about and very disorganised!

**Over the age of one, what does your child eat frequently?** Whatever we eat. We have a healthy diet with lots of fruit and veg. We are mostly vegetarian, but eat fresh fish regularly. We all like our Indian food.

**Junk food/sweets?** We don't give him sugar. I have become pretty good at making sugar-free cakes and muffins.

**What's in your medicine cupboard for the kids?** Breastmilk! I have an unopened bottle of Calpol just in case. I use paw-paw cream for skin abrasions and tea-tree oil for antiseptic.

**What is your favourite holistic treatment/ therapy?** I do believe in the healing properties of herbs, but I think exercise and healthy eating is the best form of holistic therapy.

**Sex (or lack of)?** We still bed-share with our son, so it does have an impact on our sex life, but we are both pretty happy, I think.

**Personal care?** I use a menstrual cup – a Diva cup; I think menstrual cups are the coolest. I want all my friends to get them! Of course, I haven't needed one for a while now!

**Skincare – soaps, moisturisers, sunscreen?** I like to use natural soaps, without chemicals. I occasionally moisturise, but often forget. I will always choose a natural one with no fragrance or added nasties. I have a suncreen from Australia called UV Natural which is chemical-free.

**Haircare?** I have been using rosemary shampoo and conditioner by Faith in Nature. We don't use shampoo on my son's hair, just water.

**Toothpaste?** I use Weleda Ratanhia toothpaste.

**Cosmetics?** I don't use any. I hate the feel of them on my skin, and think I look better without make-up.

**How do you deal with challenging behaviour?** I try to see that the challenging behaviour doesn't just exist in itself, but may be due to tiredness, frustration, fear, etc. Sometimes I get really frustrated though, and can snap, but I try to stay calm.

**What do you hear yourself saying to your children often that you wish you didn't?** 'Be careful!' I wasn't encouraged to take risks as a child, and I know I tend to be fearful of new experiences. I'd like to encourage my children to be sensible but not fearful.

**Do you employ childcare?** No. I can't imagine missing out on being with my child at this tender age.

**As a family, how green are you? 10 is dark and leafy, 1 is a faint hint of peppermint.** I can see that we do a lot of things that are greener than your average bear, but there is still a long way for us to go too. Maybe 7.

**Do you consider fair-trade/ethical trading?** Nearly all of my and my son's clothes are second-hand anyway. I buy fairly traded chocolate!

**What's your top eco-family tip?** Switch your electricity account over to a green supplier. Try to buy fruit and veg locally. Join with other households to buy dried food in bulk. This means you can buy organic food much more cheaply, and you can also reduce the amount of packaging required. Breastfeed! It's the cheapest way to feed your baby and better for the environment as you avoid tins of formula and sterilised bottles.

**How much TV do you/will you allow your child to watch?** We don't have a TV. I watched way too much of it as a kid and think it was a waste of time. I don't think TV shows or 'educational' computer games are really that good for children.

**Your top three tips for imperfectly natural parenting?** Breastfeeding, baby-wearing, sleep-sharing and being responsive to your baby's cues such as crying. Seek out other parents with similar values and form your own community of friendship and support. Remember that what your child eats can influence their behaviour.

**Parenting pleasures – what do you most love about being a mum?** Feeling love from my child. Knowing that I co-created a whole new human being, and that this came about as a result of love.

**What are your imperfections?** I sometimes feel that I'm not patient enough, especially when it comes to playing games with my son. I tend to get restless and want to move on to doing something 'productive' – as if spending time with my son isn't!

**Anything else you'd like to share to help towards an imperfectly natural world?** Love is the most important thing in a family, much more important than what you eat or what you wear. Life slips by very quickly. The most nourishing way to live is with a compassionate, loving heart. Having children is a great way to cultivate this love!

# Baby-proofing

'A truly appreciative child will break, lose, spoil, or fondle to death any really successful gift within a matter of minutes.'
RUSSELL LYNES

## Crawling

I've heard many a mother say proudly 'My child walked at nine months and never crawled.' We don't need to start a debate about the age at which babies should walk; mine have all walked at different ages, but there are things to be learnt from crawling.

Crawling usually starts with rolling or shuffling along and some babies 'cruise' – it doesn't really matter how. I've read that, not only does it strengthen the baby's muscles in readiness for walking, it also enhances fine and gross motor skills. The brain has to work hard to co-ordinate left with right because the hands, legs and neck need to move in synchronisation. This helps encourage brain activity and thoughts such as 'Which way shall I go now?' The senses are stimulated by exploring new things while moving across different surfaces, picking up bits of fluff and other stuff. Interestingly, the memory is also developed as the baby needs to know where he's headed and what it was he was trying to pick up. This means that, neurologically, crawling influences the ability to learn from early infancy and exercises the left/right brain connection.

When a baby starts to crawl, the most important thing is to pick up kit from the floor. Once he starts trying to pull himself up on the furniture, you'll need to make sure there is nothing reachable that could harm him, such as dangling wires or unsecured objects. I found the best way to do the baby-proofing was, literally, to get on my hands and knees and crawl around the carpet to see things from the baby's eye view, removing any potential danger.

Once babies come into your life, you can forget your lovely ornaments, trinkets and objets d'art, forget your delicate swishing curtains and low-level hi-fi and, as we found out to our cost, glass coffee tables and babies don't work well together either. The general rule is to keep things out of reach, meaning up high, put away or behind some baby-proof cupboard catches – but you don't need to go mad. As soon as my first started to explore and crawl I felt all I really needed (apart from some wire mesh over the soil of my indoor plants – he would eat the dirt!) was one very high shelf around the walls in each room.

## Playpens

I once tried a playpen for Sonny. I set it up in the middle of the room and plonked him in it with some toys, thinking he would be delighted to have his own play area. How wrong could I have been? The poor little soul stood up clutching the bars and wailed as if I'd locked him in prison! We left it there but only as a catchment area for big toys and later we decorated it and put the Christmas tree and presents in there, safe from tiny hands – now there's a great use for a playpen!

The reality, particularly if you've got more than one child, is that you do need a safe space for the older baby. Imagine he is crawling around or toddling and you're holding the new arrival in your arms. The dog barks, an alarm goes off, the doorbell rings or you hear a crashing sound. You'll need to go and see what the noise is and, while you're distracted at the door, the crawling baby or toddler will find a way of pulling the pan from the stove or the wires out of the phone. You need a safe place to leave them for a minute or two and a playpen is great for little emergencies like this. You could also section off a corner of the lounge with some cushions and a heavy chair.

## Stairgates

As a rule, I never used stairgates. They do stop children going up or falling down the stairs but, the reality is, they also stop them learning to go and up and down safely. I agree that if your stairs are very steep, uncarpeted or just above a hard stone floor, some kind of barrier is a good idea but if you've got a regular, fairly wide, carpeted staircase, once you child starts to explore the steps, let him and be just a pace behind ready to catch him if he falls. Even very young children are good at judging their own capabilities. Most will walk very carefully (even around the edge of a pool) and, once they're shown how to come downstairs backwards, there's no stopping them. 'Shock, horror!' I hear you cry. 'Has she gone stark raving mad? She's telling us to let little Frankie go up the stairs or walk by the edge of the lake!' I'm not advocating you walk away and let them wander round the swimming pool or boating lake alone, nor even climb up and down the stairs without you. You've got to be their full-time guardian angel.

## Finding a happy medium

There was a time when my husband (then partner) would wander around the house, coffee in hand, adjusting pictures on the wall if the frames were slightly crooked. He'd then stand back to view for a minute, just to make sure he'd got it right. All that changed when our second child came along. Increasingly, we started to feel that our fabulous designer house was trying to tell us something, like 'It's time to move'. It was immensely stressful living with a huge pool in the garden (the previous owners had put it in), not to mention frighteningly expensive too. Unless we built a high, gated fence, it meant we could never allow Sonny, aged eighteen months, out on the patio for a second without someone standing next to him.

We decided to sell up and swap our white house for a brown one that would still look the same after it had been crashed into by a tricycle or covered in various baby bodily fluids. We now live in a very old rambling house with a lovely safe garden and nothing much that they can damage. The toddler plays on his bike just outside the kitchen window where I can keep a watchful eye on him while I'm cleaning and preparing meals.

There's a huge difference between being there for your child all the time and being there occasionally but being fearful for his safety. It's a really bad idea to say to a child, 'Be careful near the water, you'll fall in. Don't go near the edge, you'll drown.' Far better to watch from nearby to see if you think he really is going too close, than to walk alongside and gently show him where it's best to walk. If he's climbing on to a chair (some toddlers are a bit like goats, they just need to climb on any surface they can find), rather than shouting, 'Get down, you'll fall', it's better to say gently, 'Hold tight', then guide him to a safe spot to practise his climbing.

Children who are just discovering themselves love exploring while knowing that you're nearby. Often they'll play with other children for a while or spend ages mastering a particular little challenge they've set for themselves but, every so often, they'll come running back for a cuddle. You must be there for your child but not interfere until needed.

## Letting go

I've already mentioned the fantastic book **The Continuum Concept** by Jean Liedloff, the anthropologist who has studied children in many cultures and seen how free and responsible they are at a very young age, if they're allowed to be. To be fair, some of her suggestions are a little too radical for most Western families. I didn't actually want my two-year-old holding large knives but I absolutely accept that, in the culture she was describing, the children did indeed stoke the fire and help cook the meal at the age of two. They were never alone though and everything was done as part of an extended family.

Liedloff also talks of a group of African children as young as eighteen months who were allowed to crawl near the edge of a cliff and observed each of them concentrating on finding their limits while always remaining a safe distance from danger. I can't be quite that laid back, but I did realise quite early on that I had to allow freedom in the playground, bearing in mind that it was relatively safe and not a junk yard. Once you're past that lovely age where you pop them on the baby swing and push, there comes the day when they want to go on the climbing frame by themselves. Quite frankly, your heart is in your mouth and you've usually got the engine revving ready to take them to casualty, but you have to let go.

An excellent book that explores all of this in more detail is **Do Not Disturb** by

Deborah Jackson. She bases many of her theories on Jean Liedloff but, as a British mother herself, she gives it, I feel, a more Western approach. She talks about a study done on children of varying ages in a purpose-built adventure playground. Left totally to their own devices, there were no accidents and almost no bumps or scrapes. When the parents intervened with cries of 'Be careful, don't swing too high or you'll fall', the children were much more likely to misjudge and slip or be hurt.

Both Deborah Jackson and Jean Liedloff really helped me to let go of my inherent need to do everything for my toddler. Initially, with my first child, I would grab the scissors if he picked them up and shout 'Dangerous' before whisking them away. He probably thought, 'What a fascinating reaction I get from Mummy when I grab those scary silver things – I must get them again'! I soon realised that if he was curious about the scissors I could get some paper and show him how they worked safely. Very young kids actually understand a lot more than we think and, by talking to them calmly, they pick up on our genuine concern and manage some level of understanding as to what we're on about.

If you have more than one child, you tend to become far less precious with the subsequent children as you simply cannot legislate for toys left on the stairs, marbles left within reach of the five month old and felt-tip pens (the bain of the century, if you care about your paintwork) lying around for the two-year-old to enjoy. There's no doubt that more accidents happen in the home than anywhere else and the best thing you can do is try to encourage responsible children. So my main point with safety is – be mindful. Be there in mind and body, don't over protect or rely on commercial devices, and be constantly aware. Allow them their freedom and empower them to use their instincts to detect where the dangers lie.

## Dummies

'I would never let my child use a dummy.' We all say this before we have our own children as we pass by the three-year-old 'plugged in' to a huge dummy in the supermarket. Yet how bizarre that one of the first things many of us buy for our offspring is a pacifier!

To be honest, I don't think I even considered it much. I tried a dummy in an attempt to relieve my boobs from the seemingly constant sucking, but the dummy can interfere with successful breastfeeding. If you think about it, the nearly closed mouth and pursed-lips action needed to suck on a dummy or a teat is entirely different to the wide, gaping mouth that's needed for a breast, so that's confusing for a start. Some babies will suck on a dummy, then try to transfer the same pursed lips to the breast, resulting in sore nipples and the milk supply not being stimulated.

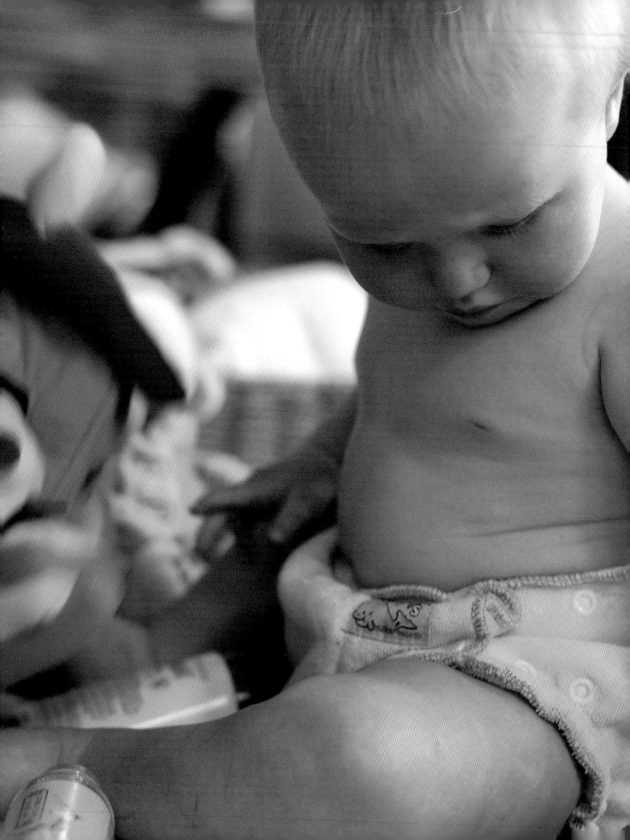

There is also the health issue around dummies. Even if we don't get too deeply into the substance they're made of and the potential for synthetic chemicals leeching from the plastic, it's almost impossible to keep a dummy clean. They're frequently dropped on the floor and we've all seen mothers pick them up and pop them straight back into the baby's mouth. I am imperfect and have, on occasion, done the classic, suck it myself then give it to the baby.

Be scrupulous about hygiene; any flexible item that goes in a baby's mouth should be sterilised, preferably in a steam steriliser, or boiled regularly. They should be replaced every four weeks at least and you should always have a clean one to hand. If you have an outbreak of thrush you'll need to replace the dummies weekly as a high percentage of them can culture yeast. Studies have also shown that long-term use of pacifiers can lead to ear infections.

Once your child is attached to them, dummies can be a devil to get rid of. If your child is addicted to his dummy, set a date not too far ahead and tell him that the dummy fairy will be winging her way to take his dummy back to the baby fairies, just like the tooth fairy. You can then creep in at night, remove the dummy and leave a little gift. As long as the child is prepared for this in advance and there are no other stressful events going on, it can be a kind of 'rite of passage'.

## Thumb sucking

There is a school of thought that says it's better to allow a child to suck on a dummy than their thumb because the dummy can be taken away. From a dental point of view, I'm told by a dentist friend that as thumbs are softer than dummies, they shouldn't cause as much malocclusion as dummies or bottle teats, as long as the baby doesn't pull on their top jaw. Of course, we must acknowledge that thumb-sucking is entirely natural and we've all seen the scan photos with the embryo sucking away.

If you have a baby who is at that full-time sucking phase, the best thing to do is offer the breast. I know you may already feel like a 24-hour milking machine and can't bear to be used as a human dummy too, but often the need to suck goes away quite quickly if the baby is given comfort. With tiny babies, I always used my own clean little finger as they seemed to quite like that. If it was obvious they didn't want the boob, I'd get DH to do the clean finger thing; it made a change for him to be the human dummy and was a pretty good indication as to whether the baby was really hungry, or simply looking for comfort.

## Teething rings

Recently, some commercially available teething rings were recalled because of the fear they may have contained bleach. Well, bleach aside, I've always wondered if the plastic itself wasn't bad enough for babies to chew on, what on earth is that fluid filling? It's usually the back teeth that bring with them the discomfort and pain, yet all the teeching rings I've seen are far too big to fit into the mouth and get at that annoying back tooth. So my advice is to think old-fashioned again. The most effective thing I found was a crunchy carrot, preferably kept in the fridge. If any of it got chewed off, all well and good – combined nutrition with teething!

If you don't feel a carrot is appropriate, the other brilliant thing is the Bickiepeg. When my mum first reminded me of these a few years ago, I assumed they would be full of sugar. Oh, doubting Thomas! Bickiepegs are teething biscuits, which were developed in 1925 by a leading paediatrician to provide the correct exercise vital to the development of a baby's jaws and teeth, with the added bonus that they ease the pain of teething. They're basically a mixture of a tiny amount of wheat with water baked to a really hard consistency and they contain no artificial sweeteners, flavourings or colouring. You can attach them to the baby's clothes with a ribbon and they kind of chew on them rather like a dog biscuit! Never leave one with your child unattended though, in case of choking. You can get them in most leading chemists or from **www.bickiepegs.co.uk**.

Teething toys are OK, particularly if you can get the eco-friendly ones that are machine washable. Teething pendants from India are said to help too (see **www.gentlebirthmethod.com**). When Lulu was born, I was given a lovely toy made with real amber beads. She enjoyed biting on that and I also found an organic cotton rabbit with eco-friendly rubberised ears that were safe for her to chew. Try **www.greenbaby.co.uk**.

## No spill cups

These are available in a multitude of designs, all in very bright plastics and mostly offering 'no spill' promises. But I was never keen on the idea of babies sucking for long periods of time on anything made of polycarbonate plastics. Studies have shown that these substances can leach potentially harmful chemicals; even so, we all buy them. I read an article saying that the average family goes through seventeen 'no spill' cups in the course of a baby's life as they always seem to get lost. It's probably a good idea to renew them frequently anyway as, when they become scratched and worn, there is greater potential for chemicals to leach into the contents. Whenever I bought a new 'sippy cup', I would look over and see my toddler happily sucking away on the one that had been lost the week before. Whatever bacteria had formed in the spout of the cup had probably grown legs by then! I always found cleaning those bits difficult.

An ordinary open cup of juice will go down in thirty seconds, unless it ends up on the floor, whereas a toddler will quite happily spend hours grazing from a 'no spill' variety. This has implications for teeth that are in prolonged contact with acidic liquids, not to mention the issues with the nature of the sucking action.

Sharon Trotter, in an article in the MIDIRS Digest, writes 'One of the many benefits of breastfeeding is its action in stimulating the muscles of the tongue and oral cavity while babies suck. This complex mechanism helps to shape the jaw and teeth and develop optimum muscle and tongue strength. When babies suck on a bottle or spout, their mouth is partially closed. Their jaw, mouth and tongue muscles are not encouraged to work as hard and, consequently, the transition to breast-feeding, after a time of bottle use, can be problematic. For this reason the World Health Organisation (WHO 2004) recommends cup feeding (open design) as the most suitable alternative, when direct breastfeeding is not possible...'

As a passionate advocate of breastfeeding, Sharon Trotter is keen to dissuade parents from using bottles, teats, spouts and lidded cups for at least the first six months. She asks whether lidded cups are even necessary or if there are implications in their use for oral health, speech and emotional development? (Sharon Trotter **www.tipslimited.com**).

Well, I 'fess up'. My second child used a trainer cup until he was nearly five and even at bedtime. Most of us know the implications of letting a child suck juice from a bottle but we somehow forget that grazing on anything sugary over a long period will have an adverse effect on a child's dental health. Some experts are now seeing this as a new risk factor among two-year-olds, referring to it as 'sucking cup caries'.

The deeper you dig into any subject, the bigger the cavity seems to get and I could go on about anecdotal evidence suggesting that many children entering pre-school are unable to drink from an open cup without spills. Speech and language therapists are seeing the normal development of the tongue and jaw muscles being delayed by spouted trainer cups, leading to possible speech difficulties.

Generally, with the kids' eating and drinking kit, I've now replaced most of the plastics with ceramics. You can get non-plastic alternatives that are dishwasher and microwave safe while being more portable than regular crockery. Try **www.baby pots.com**.

By the time I'd got to baby number four, I decided to do my best to skip the bottle stage as well as the no-spill cups. But if you're feeling overwhelmed with a sense of 'Oh no, something else I must get rid of', don't panic – we're imperfect.

## Doidy cup

Bickiepegs have made the Doidy cup, which they say is specially designed to encourage babies to drink from a rim rather than a spout. It's an excellent alternative to spouted cups made from high-density, food-grade polyethylene. The innovative design makes the cup easy for babies to use and tilt to see the contents without spilling. It is suitable for use from around three months and can eliminate the need for bottles altogether. Breastfed babies can be fed expressed milk from the Doidy cup and, after a few spills, will soon learn to drink from it. It's recommended by some health authorities and sold by the NCT. Speech and language therapists use the Doidy cup to teach lip and tongue control and it can also be used by the elderly and disabled. You can buy them in John Lewis, through the NCT or from **www.bickiepegs.co.uk**.

## Safer alternatives

The great news is that if you really can't dispense with your bottles you can now get plastic PVC-free bottles and cups from Green Baby (**www.greenbabyco.com**). They state that: 'As a company which is well aware of the potential toxic compounds that can be emitted from PVC, we all know that synthetic chemicals such as phthalates are added to make it soft and flexible.' Green Baby has a range of glass feeding bottles, PVC-free feeding cups and plates and nickel-free cutlery sets.

If you want to continue using plastic bottles but are concerned about the materials used in their manufacture, take a look at **www.babybfree.com**. This company has designed the B-Free bottle made of a new kind of plastic. They claim that, unlike most conventional bottles made from polycarbonate that can, over time become scratched and leech, theirs is made from an entirely different kind of plastic that is guaranteed to be completely free from Bisphenol A, a hormone-disrupting chemical considered to be potentially harmful to human health and the environment. They also make trainer cups that are guaranteed free of scary chemicals and their range of teats includes latex. (Be careful to check there is no latex allergy.)

## Baby signing

'First you have to teach a child to talk, then you have to teach it to be quiet.'
PROCHNOW

You'll have seen the posters in your local library and possibly, like me, you may have dismissed it as yet another new 'fad' and a way of cramming accelerated learning into your poor, overworked baby.

Baby signing is based on a programme designed by American child development expert, Joseph Garcia. There are baby signing DVDs on the market and lots of books and classes, both American and

British. I must say I haven't had the experience of anything other than a taster session with Garry Slack, a qualified British sign language tutor and founder of 'Happy Handz'. Garry says 'Research has shown that all babies use some signs, whether it is nodding or shaking their heads, waving "hello" or pointing at a favourite toy – these are natural signs understood by everyone. What is not so widely known in the UK is that, because the muscles in a child's hands develop before those needed for speech, all babies, both hearing and deaf, can be taught and encouraged to communicate with their parents and carers using sign language'.

Happy Handz shows you clearly how to communicate and learn a really worthwhile skill, albeit in its basic form initially. When Garry started to show me how to sign, I was amazed at how physical sign language is. Of course, if you're around deaf people, you'll know that to be the case. I think that, instead of sticking the kids in front of a DVD and using the TV as an electric nanny, it's fantastic to sing and sign together. Garry has found a way of incorporating the most basic signs into children's stories so that they're easy to remember. Most people start with signs such as 'food', 'more', 'all gone', 'tired'. I've been fortunate in that each of my first three children have seemed way ahead in verbal communication from a very young age (maybe because I never shut up!). Of course, it's not a competition, and speaking early isn't necessarily better, but being able to communicate somehow is very important.

We've all had our toddlers in an absolute rage because they simply can't convey their wants or needs, whether it be a drink or a cuddle. I'm told baby signing really helps and is a very worthwhile skill to learn, not just for the baby years, but beyond. It can also, in some cases, result in the child speaking at an earlier age, having an increased IQ and finding it much easier in later life to learn a foreign language. Always remember that you never sign without saying the word at the same time.

Find out more from **www.happy handz.co.uk**, **www.babysigning.co.uk** and **www.tinytalk.co.uk**.

# Toddler

Congratulations, you've made it through year one and it's likely that your baby is no longer so babyish. They'll be more mobile, toddling perhaps and, most likely starting to display a fair bit of personality, which could result in some serious tantrums (more on that later). One of the things that happens during your baby's second year is that they start becoming aware of their bodily functions.

## The birthday party

Happy first birthday! What an absolute milestone! Your cherub will no doubt be crawling, shuffling, maybe walking but definitely into everything.

The good news is that they don't yet understand the implications of a birthday party so, trust me on this one, save yourself. There'll be many more years when you'll need to invite thirty kids for a bun fight. For year one, just hole up with a bottle of champagne and a cake and celebrate your first year as a family.

Later on, when you feel the need to do the whole party thing, take these tips to be

going on with. Encourage your child to be selective; you do not need the whole nursery school wedged into your front room. Don't feel pressurised to provide 'naff' party food as healthy snacks are usually much appreciated, and don't bother with the entertainer thing until they're at least four.

Get a friend who is good at telling stories to tell a captivating one, maybe using finger puppets. Play musical chairs and sleeping lions (gives you a breather) and a final important tip – do not feel obliged to give party bags! If you feel you must send the children home with something give them each a few sunflower seeds to plant. When they grow they'll remember the friend who gave them.

## Out of nappies

I've purposely called this section 'out of nappies' rather than 'potty training' because, I must admit, the only thing my kids ever used potties for were hats!

I have a problem with the word 'training' because I don't believe you can train a baby to use a potty, or the toilet for that matter. You can guide him and encourage him to recognise when he needs to 'go' but, other than that, you're much better off waiting until he is ready, which is often later for boys than for girls.

In a way, we have made a rod for our own backs with this. With nappies, we effectively spend two to three years teaching our kids to use what they are wearing as a toilet and we are actually helping them forget their natural instinct to regulate themselves.

There is a movement known as 'Elimination Communication', popular in the United States, in which babies wear nappies for substantially less time. Apart from not being in contact with the vast amounts of chemicals in most disposables and avoiding the potential fertility issues for boys with heat in the genital area, it allows them to become more 'elimination aware', enabling them to regulate them-selves at a much earlier age. Admittedly, it requires a bit of dedication and a fair bit of holding baby's legs in the air in all manner of public places. (And poo deposited on the floor is a pretty regular occurrence.)

It's all a bit radical, even for me, but you can understand the logic behind it. It's actually the norm in many other cultures too and I often find myself taking a leaf out their books, especially when it comes to babies. I can absolutely see how it offers

more respect to babies who, apparently, can easily communicate their needs from about four months, if we are mindful of their signals.

So, when are babies ready to come out of nappies? The answer is when they want to. They're brighter than you think and they will be able to tell you. There's no correct time, so don't feel guilty if yours are later than their friends. Once they start becoming aware, don't reprimand them for accidents. By the same token, don't reward them for using the loo either, they aren't performing seals!

Let them see you on the toilet – don't be proud. Childbirth will probably have seen off any remaining inhibitions you have anyway. Our boys used to watch Dad having a pee, much to his amusement, but it was all part of the learning process for them. My first boy, Sonny, at almost three, announced one day, 'Mummy, I don't want to wear nappies any more.' He'd decided in his own time and I can't remember if it was earlier or later than I thought it would be. From then on, he happily sat on the toilet but we did need to keep him nappied up at night for a while. After a few wet beds, it was all over.

I recall outings with friends who had their portable potty dangling from their rucksack at all times, only to be amputated from their person by a closing train door. Somebody was trying to tell them something, I think! I must say, it's a whole phase I'm grateful I managed to miss.

As with so many things, use your intuition. If you try Elimination Communication, I applaud you. Check out **www.potty whisperer.com** and good luck!

## Toys and play

'A three-year-old child is a being who gets almost as much fun out of a fifty-six dollar set of swings as it does out of finding a small green worm.'

BILL VAUGHAN

Toy manufacturers are going to hate me for this but, when it comes to toys, you really don't need much. With your first child, people shower you with soft toys and plastic things with flashing lights meant to delight and stimulate. In truth, the average kitchen holds everything you need. Just dedicate a spatula, wooden spoon, a bowl, a tiny cup and teapot and most two year olds will have a ball. A baby will play for hours with a set of keys, though it's a good idea to give them their own set with safe, chewable keys; add an old mobile phone and oh, what joy

they'll have pressing those buttons! For babies and toddlers, any amount of jumping, rolling on the ground, running and splashing will bring them unlimited joy and help develop their co-ordination skills.

Most toys aren't terribly green and even I feel bad about adding to the battery mountain. Apparently, six hundred million domestic batteries, which are toxic when disposed of, are chucked out every year. It's hardly worth the guilt for the sake of a plastic teddy with a flashing nose. They're often not healthy either due to unpleasant plastics used in eighty per cent of toys. Some contain phthalates, used as plastic softeners in PVC. If you buy second-hand wooden toys, be wary of residues of toxic paint. It's paramount you check that rattles, teething toys and soft toys are non-toxic and safe. Fortunately, there are companies who stock eco-friendly toys made with organic fabrics and sustainable wood. There is plenty of exciting baby stuff at **www.toygiant.co.uk** and **www.ninnynoodlenoo.com**.

Babies and young children want to get on with the business of living and they learn

about their world through play. They love to emulate Mummy, so enlist their help with household chores. Let them use the dustpan and brush to sweep up. All of mine adore the vacuum cleaner! Toddlers love putting laundry into the machine and sorting out clean washing. So what if your socks are never in pairs again? Young children will play for hours with water too. Give them a fat paintbrush and a tub of water and let them 'paint' the outside wall or the patio. When the weather's good, a bucket, spade and a box of sand offer utopia. You don't need plastic contraptions with water on one side and sand the other; a sturdy tray of play sand is fine.

The other items you really don't need are baby walkers or those bizarre doorway baby bouncer things. The best way for a baby to find his feet is around a few low-level chairs and a little table. The toys my children enjoyed most when they were young were 'ride on'. I've got a lovely wooden rocking horse made by a local craftsman and a push-along trolley containing bricks. The boys all loved their scooters and Rocky has a car he sits in and drives with his feet, Flintstones-style.

Don't get sucked into the 'toys-must-be-educational' pitch; they don't have to be.

Toys are for playing with and life is for learning. Give your child a shoebox; he'll learn all he needs to know about shapes, sizes, aerodynamics et al. It certainly isn't worth trying to use toys to teach your children to read before they're ready. I don't think flash cards or talking letters help much and, after the initial excitement of one plastic toy with flashing lights, the novelty wears off. (By the way, will you join me in a campaign to reduce the amount of packaging and incredibly unsafe staples and wires that hold most toys in their boxes?) Most educational toys aimed at young kids are simply a way of making parents feel good. However, I did once get an inflatable globe that did us proud.

If you're pushed for space or on a tight budget, do yourself a favour, and don't buy any toys for your new baby. Chances are they'll have lots bought by friends and relatives. Do make sure there's a wide range of fun stuff for him to play with and borrow toys from your local toy library. These are fantastic places where for a couple of pounds, you can hire great toys for a fortnight. If there are any your child really enjoys, renew them or look to acquiring them from eBay or Freecycle (**www.uk.freecycle.org**).

If you think I'm being a killjoy and you'd like to buy some good-quality, brand-new toys, there are some wonderful eco-friendly things available, which are fair trade too, from **www.holz-toys.co.uk**.

I've also come across another work-at-home mum who set up a company offering unusual wooden, educational, soft and traditional toys and high-quality products, hand-selected from around the world. They'll create an account for you online for wealthy relatives to view your child's wish list (I wish!). See **www.anara.co.uk**. There are some brilliant solar-powered toys, including a lovely helicopter, at **www.nigelsecostore.co.uk**.

### Toddler's Property Laws
If I like it, it's mine.

If it's in my hand, it's mine.

If I can take it from you, it's mine.

If I had it a little while ago, it's mine.

If it's mine, it must never appear to be yours in any way.

If I am doing or building something, all the pieces are mine.

If it looks like mine, it is mine.

If I saw it first, it's mine.

If you are playing with something and you put it down, it automatically becomes mine.

..........If it's broken, it's yours.

## Books

Books are an entirely different issue – you can't have too many of them. Check out your local charity shops and do join the library, where there's usually a fantastic range for toddlers and children. Some organise a communal story-time that offers a great introduction to sitting with other children. (Mine often took the opportunity to have afternoon naps!)

When you look through a book with your children, it should be a tactile experience, so buy board or fabric ones when they're babies. You'll probably find they want to hear the same story over and over again. With my boys, the classic **Peepo!** by Janet and Allan Ahlberg was an

terms anything that might be worrying him. If he's not feeling well, for example, make up a story about a teddy that was poorly but soon felt better. When you are reading at bedtime and once they have playmates, it's nice to remember their names and say 'God bless' to each of them. If you have a Christian faith, you might like to use some of the lovely children's prayer books that are available too.

One of the nicest online stores for books is **www.barefoot-books.com**. Their strapline is 'Celebrating art and story'.

## Craft stuff

It's great to get the kids involved in arts and crafts at an early age. They're often happy to paint with just water on paper and walls but, once you add colour, make sure the paint is non-toxic. A gorgeous set of water-based colours is available from **www.myriadonline.co.uk**, where there is also a wide range of natural art materials, all with non-toxic dyes. You can buy some lovely organic craft materials and soft toys such as organic wool felt juggling balls from **www.greenfibres.com**.

Playdough and clay are fantastic for early modelling activities. You can even make

absolute winner. It's probably a bit 'un pc' now, with Mummy cleaning the windows and Grandma doing the ironing, but it is a beautiful first book. Rocky was a huge fan of the Maisy series and all the boys love the Percy the Park Keeper stories by Nick Butterworth.

One of the most rewarding experiences you'll have as parents is reading stories to your kids. Make some up as well. Don't worry if you aren't an aspiring novel writer, as the simplest tale will delight them. It's a great idea to offer a story that recounts the experiences of the day. You can talk about your child almost as if he isn't there: 'Once upon a time, there was a little boy called Rocky. He had a lovely day playing with his brothers and his baby sister.' This can be a great way to sort out in simplistic your own play-dough using the following recipe – it's edible, though consumption is not advised!

## Playdough

450g/1 lb bicarbonate
   of soda
1 cup of cornstarch
1 cup of cold water
Add a couple of drops of
   food colouring if you want
   it to look pretty.

### Method

Mix the ingredients in a pan, then simmer slowly on the hob, stirring continuously. Mash it up until it feels like mashed potato and leave to cool. Lay it out on a tray or board and cover with a damp cloth. When it's cool, knead to form a ball. It can be stored in a plastic bag in the fridge for up to a week.

You and your children can make a veritable array of candleholders, dinosaurs, robots or other favourite items or characters, or simply use a pastry cutter and make funky shapes. It air-dries in a couple of days, or bake in an oven on a very low heat for about ten minutes. It can then be decorated with poster paints to create fabulous gifts. Alternatively you can use coloured beeswax

(you'll need to warm it up before you mould it). You can get modelling beeswax and beautiful beeswax crayons made by Stockmar from Myriad as above.

## Dressing up

A cheap and simple idea is to make a dressing-up box. Sort through your bric-a-brac and donate the shiny, interesting bits to the dressing-up box. Kids turn old bits of fabric into capes, crowns and even ball gowns. Charity shops hold endless delights.

## Music

All children love music and sounds. They also love beat, though they don't necessarily have much rhythm. Newborn babies adore the sound of their mother's voice and that's why singing to your baby can be so soothing, even if you think you have an awful singing voice. You may also have heard of the so-called 'Mozart effect', which suggests that babies who listen to classical music will be brighter than those brought up on the Rolling Stones and Brit pop. You'll need to show me a lot more research before I'll buy that one! My view is, make music fun for its own sake. Play music, sing nursery rhymes, make up little rhymes and sing with your children; get a wooden spoon, bang a saucepan and chill-out! It's not essential to buy your toddler electronic keyboards with bells and whistles. Singing and doing the actions to kiddies' songs will make you feel downright daft at first but you'll soon see the delight on the face of your toddler (and sniggering partner) and it will be worth it.

## Television and videos

This is not the place for a rant about kids watching TV. The truth is, I'm very imperfect on this one. I don't actually practise what I preach. My principle is that children under three shouldn't be exposed to TV screens or computers, whatever the programme content. I just believe it's not great for them to be involved in passive activity. Watching television does not require any practice of the fine or gross motor skills, co-ordination, communication or creativity.

I can't advocate using the telly as an 'electric nanny' but we've all done it to buy an hour or two. If they are watching it, however, do try to do something in the same room. With the first child, it's easy because you just don't have to turn it on. What he doesn't know about, he can't hanker after. By the time he has little friends and they're all watching the Tellytubbies, you can't help

but get caught up in it all. You may well be able to hold out until they are three but, with subsequent children, there's no hope. Buddy, my second boy, wanted to do what his big brother was doing and one of his first phrases at fifteen months was 'Rosie and Jim'!

Rocky, my third little boy, was asking for 'Cinderbrella' by the age of two because he'd seen his big brother watching it, so I'm in no position to lecture you. I can only say, limit it in the early years. Until they were about four, I would only let them watch videos in order to monitor the content and avoid the pester power of advertising. Even some kids' shows are a bit dodgy and I limited viewing to under an hour a day. As the boys got older and wanted to watch TV shows, I tried to time it so that the toddler was in bed or I'd video the programme.

Even imperfectly natural opinions conflict on this. I have friends who are way more natural than I am but, when it comes to the TV, they really believe it's entertaining, educational and can do no harm. Some take it one stage further and reckon any TV is fine if you sit and watch it with your kids and discuss it, but I also have several friends who have never had a TV in the house and their kids are fantastic at coming up with inventive, imaginative things to do. They do get a bit of TV at friends' houses, so the jury's out on this one! I'd say trust your instincts.

# Good food
# for mother
# and baby

'Those who think they have no time for healthy eating
will sooner or later have to find the time for illness.'
EDWARD STANLEY

Many children's problems can be attributed to dietary issues. I've witnessed children with debilitating conditions, from autism and attention deficit disorders to hyperactivity, being turned around by simple changes in diet. Bad behaviour or naughtiness can often indicate the body's attempt to communicate an underlying deficiency. If there are issues with your child – psychological or physical – look at their nutrition first. With children, it is often as simple as 'you are what you eat'. See a good nutritionist if you can and, remember, if you were deficient during pregnancy or at the time of your child's birth, this could have had an impact.

Young children need a good balance of all the vital nutrients in fresh healthy food, including calcium, magnesium, potassium and zinc. It's so interesting that colostrum, that rich, first breast milk that lasts for around four days after birth, contains about six months' supply of zinc, after which the baby can get it from foods, as long as they're able to absorb it properly. Nature is so clever. If sodium is present in young children's foods, it will not aid absorption of much-needed nutrients. We consume far too much salt ourselves, so it's a good opportunity to cut down. From your child's point of view, what they haven't had, they won't miss.

If you suspect deficiencies or intolerances, it's a good idea to see a qualified nutritional therapist (**www.bant.org.uk**). A great website for more information is by 'The Food Doctor' Ian Barr. (**www.the fooddoctor.com**). He is also the author of some excellent books on nutrition.

I could list all the foods to give your baby but we all know what they should or shouldn't be eating, don't we? Fresh, organic, unprocessed, locally sourced food with no additives. This can be hard to achieve, I know, but that's the ideal. The imperfectly natural concept is to get as close to that as you can.

What we eat – our nutrition – is the single most important thing we can get right. Most people still don't really understand the direct equation between what we put into our bodies and what happens to us as a consequence.

There are a million books on the subject, including my own first book **Imperfectly Natural Woman**. I can't cover it all here but, for the basics, let's look at what's going to concern us now that we have a new precious little person to feed. First, let's start with where to get the best food.

## Supermarkets

Ideally, we'd all grow our own vegetables, make our own bread and cakes, and get our fruit and groceries from local organic farmers' markets or from organic box deliveries. But, let's face it, we love our supermarkets. Imperfect as I am, I'm always going to need them and, to be honest, a visit to a good supermarket can be quite therapeutic. There are some things that supermarkets do really well, so here's a quick 'guide to the aisles' and how to utilise them in our imperfectly natural lives.

Wherever possible, buy British and organic, especially when it comes to fruit and veg. Look for unpackaged, fresh food that has travelled the least number of miles. Some supermarkets are now offering organic vegetable boxes. Having said that, the supermarkets are excellent at introducing us to exotic fruits, so try out some kumquats and star fruit, and enjoy!

Lobby the supermarkets to stock products from independent companies. Often I've found my favourite brands have disappeared off the shelves (the brilliant Whole Earth company and Baby Organix jars spring to mind), to be replaced by supermarket organic 'own brands'. Ask customer services to restock them. If enough people ask, they will respond. Get used to looking at the ingredients on everything.

You can pretty much rely on supermarkets for organic, high-quality store cupboard goods including nuts, pulses and grains (even more unusual ones like quinoa). The selection of breakfast cereals is usually good – just scurry past the brightly coloured branded stuff with free toys and get to the organic range.

Most supermarket bakeries offer a decent organic loaf; order it specially, if that's what you want. They usually have a fairly comprehensive wheat- and gluten-free range, including the excellent Terence Stamp collection of wheat-free breads (yes, the actor with the gorgeous blue eyes). Don't be fooled into thinking that, just because something is wheat-free, it is necessarily healthy. Some include a huge amount of preservatives, sugar or chemical sweeteners, salt and fat, including hydrogenated vegetable oils which, let's face it, aren't needed in a jam tart.

Some supermarkets have great salad bars and delicatessen counters. Often it will be the only one for miles around as there are so few independent ones now. It's a good way to try small amounts of different olives, cheeses, pâtés and other goodies. Most offer good organic, vegetarian and sheep's and goat's cheese. I don't think I'd have ever have tried halloumi cheese if my supermarket hadn't been offering a few little barbecued taster samples. Now I love it. The dairy section should be well stocked with organic eggs and milk.

More on the meat debate later (see page 119), but it's clearly not possible to know your cow when it's packaged up on supermarket shelves. If you need to buy meat and poultry there, look for British-reared, always organic and certified by the Soil Association. That way you can at least ensure that the organic status has been adhered to.

If your supermarket has a fresh fish counter, ask your fishmonger to order in and prepare your favourite fish, particularly if it's something more unusual like swordfish. You'll get the freshest fish that way and he'll let you know when a really good catch is coming in. If he's knowledgeable, chat to him about sustainability too and favourite recipes.

One thing the supermarkets are hot on is baby foods and drinks, and fortunately there are some excellent healthy options for kids. So many of the brightly coloured packages aimed at attracting kids are the products that contain the worst ingredients. It's getting better though; Asda and a couple of other supermarkets now stock some of the more natural ranges aimed at children such as the fantastic Organic Pasta in the shapes of the characters from The Simpsons (an uncannily precise Bart!) and it's easy to find 100 per cent organic smoothies, for example those from Ella's Kitchen, and the squeezable fruit pouches from Kali Bio. Some supermarkets also stock Supajus, orange juice or apple and blackberry fortified with fish oils – and no, you really can't taste it! I can't fault supermarkets on their selection of herb teas or wines either, as most have an excellent, small, reasonably priced, organic range. Perhaps most importantly, supermarkets have great chocolate. Most now stock the fair-trade Divine chocolate bars and drinks.

In the cleaning department, the supermarkets have listened to the consumer, I think, and usually stock a range of eco-friendly cleaning equipment, the big players as well as their own brands. A few stock eco-disposable nappies and a couple of high-street chemists even have a small stock of cloth nappies. Microfibre cloths are available and you can pick up the lemons, white vinegar and, occasionally, borax and large packets of bicarbonate of soda you need for making your own cleaners. Sadly, none stocks soapnuts or laundry balls – yet!

As a rule, supermarkets and high street chains will generally respond to consistent consumer demands so, if we want fresh, good quality, healthy and organic foods as well as fairly traded ethical products, that's what they'll give us. If the organic ranges don't sell, they'll take them off the shelves. So much rides on our awareness of the whole food quality issue and, as we become more discerning over what we put on and in our bodies, the supermarkets will follow our lead. They're not there yet, but they're making great strides. Let's all agree to badger them about packaging too: reduce–reuse–recycle is my mantra!

# Organic?

It's such a trendy buzzword and one that I'm guilty of bandying around incessantly. Don't get me wrong, I still believe that the foods we eat should be organic but what does 'organic' actually mean? I have an apple tree in my garden, which to the best of my knowledge has never seen a chemical spray or fertiliser in its life. If I were to pick a box of apples from it and sell them at a local market with the word 'organic' displayed, I would be breaking the law. This is a problem for many small local producers, as the cost of achieving organic status is high and many are simply not earning enough to pay for the certification. Often these are small growers whose produce is genuinely organic.

When we speak now of an organic vegetable, usually we assume that means it's been grown like my apples. Possibly it has, but 'certified organic' doesn't necessarily mean pure. At its worst, it could mean that the organic fruits that are so beautifully packaged and flown in from abroad were grown using only fifteen different types of chemicals instead of the usual twenty-five. Also, it may have been sitting around for weeks in cold storage, or on the sides of polluted roads, quickly losing much of its nutritional value. Okay, I'm being slightly facetious here, but organic certification procedures appear to vary greatly and if, you look into the requirements for a food achieving organic status, you may ask yourself whether the guidelines are stringent enough or even what you thought they were, or whether we are paying a high premium for foods that are deemed the best merely because they display that little organic sticker.

# Local produce

It's not just the growing that counts, it's also important where and when the produce was grown. Our bodies were designed to eat seasonally. I don't want polytunnels all over the country to give me strawberries in winter because I don't need strawberries in winter. It's important to know how long they were stored for, where and in what conditions. A label saying 'British grown' doesn't mean much at all. Some retailers fly British mushrooms to Poland for washing and packing, then back again ready for the shelves. Hardly green, I'd say.

Fortunately, many of us are wising up to all of this, hence the growth of farmers' markets and local vegetable box schemes. I use the excellent Riverford Organics (**www.riverford.co.uk**).

The phrase that's become trendier than organic is 'locally sourced', meaning grown by small-scale businesses and growers. I went to my local farmers' market recently and saw a stall overflowing with the most vibrantly colourful fruit and vegetables I'd ever seen. The stallholder told me: 'We aren't allowed to class it as organic because we can't afford to pay for certification, in truth it would take our profits away. What we can tell you is that it is, in fact, more organic than most certified organic vegetables. It's grown on our own farm in Cambridgeshire, was picked only yesterday and absolutely nothing has been sprayed on it. We buy insects to fend off vegetable-eating bugs'. It was some of the best-tasting veg I've had. Grown in season, without chemicals and within thirty miles of my home and with no storage time, it was served up on my table within twenty-four hours of being picked.

Most towns and cities now have a regular farmers' market. Sadly, like mine, they're usually only held once a month, but if there is enough demand perhaps that will increase. Contact your local council to see whether there is one in your area. Most sell a few craft items alongside the usual stalls selling home-grown veg, jams, cheeses, breads and cakes, herbal products, free range eggs and locally produced meat. Talk to the sellers and ask them if any chemicals have been used in their growing process. To find a market near you, try **www.local-farmers-markets.co.uk/ contact.html** or the National Association of Farmers' Markets (**www.farmersmarkets. net**) You can also join Friends of Local Foods at **www.farma.org.uk**.

If you're lucky enough to have a great health shop near you that sells local and organic produce, try to support them. If you have a local 'Fresh and Wild' or a 'Planet Organic', you'll have a wealth of choice. There are an increasing number of brilliant, independent stores which really embrace the healthy and sustainable message (**www.cooksdelight.co.uk**).

There are quite a few companies springing up with all this in mind and one of my

favourites is The Ethical Food Company (**www.ethicalfoodcompany.co.uk**), which sells a full range of locally sourced food and drink. As a supplier, they are certified by the Soil Association. One might assume then that all their produce is certified organic, but it isn't. They are looking at a much wider picture, which relates not just to the fact that someone has managed to label their product organic but that it is local, seasonal, extremely high quality, fairly traded and produced to high animal welfare standards where applicable.

The bottom line is, eat as healthy a diet as you can, give or take some imperfections of course. Most of the food you eat should be unprocessed and, wherever possible, grown without the use of too many synthetic chemicals. Look behind the label and find out where the food is grown and in what conditions. When it comes to what's on your dinner table, 'Think global, act local'. Get to know the source of your meat and vegetables before they arrive on your plate. There's lots of information at **www.aboutorganics.co.uk**.

## Grow your own

The best way to know your vegetables is to grow your own. Gardening is the new rock and roll and it's a great stress reliever. It keeps you in tune with nature, and toddlers love it. Give a two-year-old a trowel and a little watering can and you've got a couple of hours of blissful entertainment sorted. We used to have a gardener who, to be honest, wasn't actually that good. We kept him on because the moment he arrived, my three-year-old and four-year-old would rush out to see him and they would all potter around in the garden while he did his work – allegedly. Gardening and childcare rolled into one!

If you're not the green-fingered type, don't think you have to spend Sundays in garden centres sourcing organic seedlings; many don't stock them anyway. I've got a fantastic imperfectly natural solution for you. Buy yourself an 'Instant Organic Vegetable Garden'. The wonderfully named Mike Kitchen from Rocket Gardens emailed me to offer me one of these and I almost bit his hand off. I'm a busy girl and I don't have time to go and buy organic plants, let alone dig the patch. Mike suggested an instant vegetable garden that can be planted in among the flowers and plants already there, perfect for stupidly busy cheats like me. We got strawberries, herbs, all manner of salad things, tomatoes, courgettes, aubergines, broccoli, beans and loads more, all organically grown and packed in little biodegradable pots that the kids popped into the ground with ease. They had such fun and even little Rocky, at two, remembered to take his watering can and water the plants every day. It was great to see him connecting with nature. Hopefully he won't be one of those eleven year olds who doesn't know where a courgette comes from! You can get kitchen veg and herb gardens from **www.rocket**

gardens.co.uk. Watch out for the slugs though. You don't need any chemical slug repellents. Just sprinkle some broken eggshells around the plants as they don't like to slither over them. Or try porridge oats – the slugs eat them, the oats expand and kill them (sorry about cruelty to slugs).

# Food and nutrition for healthy children

## Weaning and first foods

The official line on when a baby should be weaned, or rather start eating solids in addition to milk, seems to change with the wind. The current recommended time is four to six months but I'm not suggesting that you necessarily go with the official recommendations. Giving a baby solids before four months can result in colic and constipation, and lead to greater food intolerances as the baby's digestive system isn't developed enough to cope. Also, if you reduce the amount of breast milk in favour of solid food, your baby will be missing out on vital nutrients and antibodies.

My own feeling is that you must trust your intuition. If all was perfect, we should aim for six months of exclusive breastfeeding but, the reality is that I've done slightly less than that with mine. Some babies go to seven or eight months, or even up to a year on purely breast milk and seem to do just fine. The important thing is not to beat yourself up about it; there is no right or wrong. You haven't failed because your strapping hungry baby wants to grab a roast potato off your plate at four and a half months.

## How do you know when they're ready for food?

It's important to recognise the signs and then to introduce foods slowly. Try to sense when they're ready. They'll probably start to show a keen interest in the food on your plate, wondering if they're missing out on something. Often they will demand more breastfeeds or seem to be hungry and grizzly after a feed, although that could just be growth spurt. It does no harm to give them a tiny taste of something unseasoned and it's wonderful to watch the look on their face when their taste buds are aroused for the first time.

Baby-led weaning is my best tip here. Basically, it's a way of letting the baby choose when he's ready and giving him mostly what the family eat. By doing this, some people manage to avoid altogether the pureed food stage. All they need to start with are organic vegetables and fruit, mostly as finger foods, such as well cooked but not mushy broccoli with stems, potato wedges, roast carrot and parsnip in chunks.

As your baby gets to about month nine or ten he can tolerate a wider range of foods. I introduced live yoghurt sweetened with a bit of fresh fruit. At this point they can have fruit with seeds such as raspberries and blackberries. Mine all wanted to hold their own food at this stage and you start to wonder how you'll get anything healthy other than a carrot stick into them without a spoon, so, for this phase get a copy of the excellent book **Finger Foods for Babies and Toddlers** by Jennie Maizels (Vermilion). It offers great suggestions.

Many people recommend you start with a little baby rice mixed with breast milk but none of mine would touch it. I used organic brown rice formed into balls and another option is to use quinoa (cook it like rice). Remember that they are still getting most of their nutrition from breast milk or formula at this point. There are official recommendations as to the amount of breast milk babies should be getting at this time but, if you breastfeed on demand as I have done, you've absolutely no idea how much they take at each feed.

## Commercial baby foods

However lovingly you wash, peel and chop those organic carrots, slave over a hot stove, cooking and cooling before puréeing or blending to a fine consistency, your baby will eat your offering with trepidation and probably spit some out. When on the hop one day, you head off to the park and grab a jar of organic carrot, your baby will wolf it down as though he hasn't had any grub in weeks. I don't know why this is, it just is. The good news is that there is excellent baby food on offer now. Perhaps the finest of the jar options is the Holle range, which you can get at **www.ulula.co.uk**. They claim to be the first company to offer biodynamically sourced and grown organic baby foods.

Baby Organix (**www.organix.com**) is one of my favourite UK brands. They also do a great range of dried food, including organic baby breadsticks and little animal-shaped biscuits. Hipp is available in most supermarkets, but is not always 100 per cent organic. If you can get them, BabyNat make fabulous vegetarian baby food imported from France (**www.goodness direct.co.uk**).

Ella's Kitchen makes pure organic fruit and vegetables in little re-sealable squeezy pouches. They are available from Waitrose, Sainsbury's and some branches of Holland and Barrett.

## Freezing your own

If you want puréed food, make it yourself and you'll know it's organic and fresh. All you need is a hand blender and some ice-cube trays. If you're too imperfect for that, Truly Scrumptious make baby food freshly frozen in individual portions. They have twice won the coveted Soil Association Organic Babyfood Award. They also make organic unseasoned stock so baby can share your dinner! **www.bathorganic**

**babyfood.co.uk**. Some supermarkets are now making their own ranges as well.

For more information, I love **What Should I feed My Baby? The Complete Nutrition Guide from Birth to Two Years** by Susannah Olivier (Weidenfeld and Nicholson). She has some great suggestions as to what babies should eat, how to start feeding them and exactly what their nutritional needs are, from essential fatty acids to proteins. There are also loads of easy recipes for every stage up to two years and a great section on 'Remedies for Common Ailments'.

It's still best to avoid salt, sugar (apart from fruit sugars, of course), eggs and very high fibre foods that could cause bloating and discomfort. Your baby can probably eat a meal every three to four hours and snacks aren't usually needed at this stage. Fat definitely is though, so if you're on a low-fat diet yourself, don't think that's okay for the baby. They need a good level of essential fatty acids. You can also give water to drink as well as breast milk but it should be as well as, not instead of.

Just a word about snacks and eating on the run. I steered away from the commercial snack foods as I found my baby was just as happy with a slice of red pepper or a carrot to chew on. Bananas and avocados make great natural fast foods for babies over six months. Just slice open a ripe avocado and spoon it out. Like olives, which babies also love, they're almost a complete food on their own, with protein, vitamins, minerals and carbohydrate all packed into one.

In the old days, you were probably given rusks to teethe on. These are not great as they contain sugar. Enter rice cakes, healthy bite-size treats. Get the organic ones with no salt or flavourings.

Mealtimes can be fun, as long as you don't mind you and the kitchen walls being covered in baby food, which does make for some great photos. For the times when you've kitted them out in their Sunday best, you can get some very substantial bibs but the simple, cheap Velcro ones worked best for me. Remember to fasten them before putting them in the washing machine to prevent the Velcro losing its stickiness. If you're into designer bibs, check out Lulu's 'I Want Chips Chocolate and Cake' from **www.snuglo.com**.

## Mealtimes

Rigid sit-down mealtimes are unlikely to work for infants. If you have a child who isn't a fan of eating, be creative, make it a game, be cowboys and imagine a campfire, put on hats and cook beans along with your vegetables. My favourite game is the train spoon going 'chuff chuff' into the tunnel – it always gets a laugh. Another is to sit on the patio as the child does laps round the table in a toy car. Every time he rides past he stops to fill up with petrol and has a mouthful. He may not manage to swallow it by the next pit stop, but it's a start.

As my son got older, I started to include him in family mealtimes and to give him chopped up bits of what we were all eating. I often found that he would have his own routine and timescale for eating dinner, however. Toddlers sometimes like to pick and will span a meal over an hour or so. Try not to clear up immediately after everyone else has wolfed down their food. He could easily toddle back and forth for an hour or two, snacking on bits of his dinner. We occasionally put a pudding out at the same time too and that might go first. The point is, you don't mind how or when, as long as they eat.

If your child is picky, try to work out your strategy with your partner or whoever looks after your children when you aren't around. If they get too many confusing messages they'll play one of you off against the other and it could be the beginning of a lifetime of fussy eating.

## Providing healthy choices

Children can be quite self-regulating and if they eat very little at one meal they'll make up for it at snack time or at the next meal, so it really is about keeping a variety of healthy choices in the cupboard. In order to get your children to eat a wide range of foods you will need, at least initially, to be creative and, some say,

sneaky. Fresh fruit and vegetables can easily be blended into 'smoothies'. Linseed, hemp, sunflower and pumpkin seeds can be ground up and added to the bread maker or sprinkled over cereals. Toddlers love food they eat with their fingers so it's all about presentation. Of course, toast must always be 'soldiers'.

With older children, it's a bit harder. Their taste buds are pretty refined and they may well hit the roof if they think they've been fooled into eating a carrot. I'm convinced that's one of the reasons that so many children like really bland foods. They want their pasta without sauce and flatly refuse soup or casseroles in case something indefinable gets 'snuck in'. Any food that has not been tried before is regarded as, at best, suspect and, at worst, poison.

Once children start eating out at other people's houses, parties or in cafés, the fun really starts. We rather foolishly thought that, as we were vegetarian, our kids would be too – mistake! When my first son was about ten months old we were at a buffet-style party and I was carrying him in a sling. As I bent down to put some celery sticks on our plate his eyes fixed on a plate of ham slices and he lunged out and grabbed a handful. He promptly ate the lot, giggling delightedly. Now, at seven, it's clear he absolutely loves and seems to need meat, as do his brothers.

# Imperfectly natural parent

**Your name, age group, age of children** Mandy, aged 27, and my children are two and four.

**Occupation?** I previously worked as a deputy manager for Unwins Wine Merchants with my husband, who was branch manager. It was handy because we lived above the shop, so if my son needed a feed, my husband would bring him down to me, and then serve the customers, while my son contentedly latched on to me!

When my second son, George was born, I decided it was time to be full-time mum to my two children. I took a year's maternity leave before deciding to resign. I spent time on eBay, buying second-hand clothes for my children and I became a seller myself. Then I decided it would be a good idea to promote breastfeeding on eBay. Originally, my business www.laitdamour.com was a hobby, but I soon became bombarded with friendly emails and other websites requesting wholesale Nursing Necklaces and Booby Reminder® bracelets!

**Birth experiences – natural /assisted?** During the birth of my first son, James, I got through with gas and air. After the birth, I had a retained placenta and was taken to theatre where I was given a spinal block for a manual removal. I had hoped for a completely natural birth, but it doesn't always go to plan!

**Your emotional state for the first six months?** When my first son was born, I was overly protective of him. I felt on edge when anyone held him, and I would never let him out of my sight. I'd even wheel his crib into the bathroom so I could be near him.

When my second son was born, I had difficulties bonding with him at first, and I was assessed by my health visitor as suffering post-natal depression. Through breastfeeding, I was able to establish a bond with my son naturally, with skin-to-skin contact and the reassurance of knowing I was doing well for him.

**When did your figure return? Did you exercise?** No, I never exercised, other than pelvic floor exercises after the birth of my second son. I'm not one to worry about my shape, as long as I am eating healthily. Breastfeeding helped my weight return to normal by about six months postpartum.

**How was your relationship with your partner?** My husband supported me and our new family; he actually encouraged co-sleeping when my first son wouldn't settle at night. He was very supportive of breastfeeding too! He's an 'imperfectly natural' dad!

**Breastfeeding experience?** Amazing! Very rewarding to know you do not only grow your baby inside you, but in fact you can continue to grow that baby with your body, producing milk which is designed specifically for your own child! Nothing compares with the benefits of human milk!

**First foods – homemade purées or jars?** I started with baby rice, and pureed fruits and vegetables. I mostly made my own, following baby recipe books and my own experimentation – but yes, I did use the occasional jarred baby food! My first son actually went off solids after a while, in preference for my milk. I never pushed the issue, just went with the flow, but I do feel I was pressured by the health visitor to introduce solids too early, so it could go in that 'little red book'! (At the time, the introduction of solids was recommended at four months.) But in practice, James never really got into solids until aged 12 months because my milk sustained him.

As he grew older, he became a 'fussy' eater (like my husband), he reacted to dairy products and was sick with milk, eggs and cheese.

**Junk food/sweets?** Sweets as a treat only. But when they are at a birthday party, I won't be too hard on them! I think if you are too limiting they grow up to 'pig out' on sweets, because they have been restricted in the past.

I think healthy eating starts at the shops! If you buy junk food then that's what you and your child will eat at home!

With a little thought and inspiration, it's amazing what you can cook up! Even if you do disguise the vegetables!

**What's in your medicine cupboard for the kids?** Plasters, bandages, Calpol, arnica cream, TCP, Karvel vaporiser, Eucalyptus oil and more…

**What do you do to keep 'sane'? What do you do for 'me' time?** It is only recently, as my children are growing older, that I can think more about myself and what I intend to do in the future. Later this year I will be studying counselling skills while my children are at pre-school. Knowing I could help others gives me much satisfaction and self-esteem.

**What is your favourite holistic treatment/therapy?** Spirituality – going to my local church 'All Saints'.

**Sleep (or lack of)?** When my first son was born and was in a crib, he woke constantly. By week two, I decided to follow my instincts and take him to bed with me. The night feeds were so easy, I'd just roll over and then we'd both fall back to sleep.

**How do you get exercise?** Mostly from going out for walks with the children and the dog.

**How do you deal with challenging behaviour?** For young children, I believe challenging behaviour arises because of their lack of ability to communicate, so talking to them and trying to understand their frustrations. 'Time out' seems to be effective too.

**What do you hear yourself saying to your children often that you wish you didn't?** 'Get out', when I am trying to take a phone call and the noise level is horrendous. Don't you find they 'play up' when you're on the phone?

**As a family, how green are you? 10 is dark and leafy, 1 is a faint hint of peppermint** About a 4 I'd say, but we're still learning! Can't wait to read **Imperfectly Natural Baby and Toddler** for more tips!

**Do you recycle everything?** Almost everything, yes! We go to the recycling bins every week.

**How much TV do you/will you allow your child to watch?** About an hour whilst I get ready in the mornings and get their breakfast prepared.

**How do you feel about commercial toys and branding? Are you first in the queue at midnight on Christmas Eve for this year's must-have toy?** No way! Quite the opposite, in fact – brand names and advertising have no effect on our family. We always purchase sensibly.

**Your top three tips for imperfectly natural parenting?** Follow your instincts. Breastfeed (on demand too!). Co-sleep.

As a very general guideline, most pre-school children, as well as those at school, need fruit juice on waking to replace their blood sugar levels. Then they need a decent, filling breakfast, a small snack mid-morning, lunch between 12 and 1 p.m., a light mid-afternoon snack and dinner between 5 and 6 p.m. Over threes may need another small snack before going to bed.

## Fruit and vegetables

If you really want to eat well as a family, a great way to encourage the kids is with a wall chart and, if the food looks colourful, you're halfway there. The Rainbow Food Activity Chart for children (and adults!) helps to ensure they have their daily intake of the nutritious food colour groups in the recommended five portions a day. Each colour group includes fruit and vegetables. At the end of the week, stickers can be given to the ones who have covered all the colours for each day of the week. It's a fantastic way of reminding Dad to eat his greens too! The chart has been beautifully hand-drawn to make it especially attractive to children and it's laminated so it doesn't get too mucky! Get it from **www.lemonburst.co.uk**.

## Snacks

Toddlers often need small meals, little and often, so provide healthy snacks and finger foods like rice cakes and humous, raisins or pieces of apple or pear. Steer well clear of biscuits and cakes laden with sugar and hydrogenated vegetable oil. Fortunately, there are some great healthy snack bars in supermarkets now, including the Bounce snack and Trek natural energy bars.

## Cooking with kids

Cooking with kids is a fantastic way of encouraging them to eat their food. Get them involved in the whole process. Even little children can help in the supermarket – ask them to get a nice big lettuce or cucumber. Start by letting them help make a sandwich and progress to greater things.

When your little one is desperate to stand up at the work surface with you, you are likely to find that a chair is not exactly ideal. Consider, then, The FunPod, an innovative bit of furniture that looks like a 'tower' of wood. The kids look a bit like they're safe in their own little castle, while

they stand next to you helping with the chores. It's designed for children aged one to four and comes flat packed from **www.littlehelper.co.uk**.

# The sugar rush

'Inside me lives a skinny woman crying to get out. But I can usually shut her up with cookies.'

ANON

## Feeling guilty?

When it comes to sweets, it's easy for me to write about the ideals – but I don't put it all into practice. My boys go on days out to the park, beach trips, even camping holidays when a homemade anything, let alone a nice fresh fruit ice lolly, is a pipe dream. The idea of offering a healthy cereal bar or dried fruit snack is laughable on these occasions when all their friends are eating a bag of crisps.

There are times when you have to retreat and go with the flow. Just have the ideals in the back of your mind so that you can at least aim for the 80/20 principle. One of my dear friends has a good rule for the whole family. They eat only organic, very wholesome, decent meals and snacks when they're at home. There is absolutely no rubbish bought or kept in the house, so there's no temptation. When they go on outings or to friends' houses, the kids choose whatever they want and are allowed to accept treats if offered. She feels it balances out beautifully. Interestingly, you'd think her children aged six and nine would be craving sweet stuff and would greedily grab everything going when they visit friends. The opposite is true; they haven't ever developed a sweet tooth. Both children have excellent teeth and have not needed any fillings or dental work, whereas my second child needed a small filling at five years of age. I beat myself up!

## Sweets and cakes

If you've only just given birth to your first child, you may be horrified that I'm even discussing sweets while claiming to care about my children's health. My first son didn't get even a sniff of sugar mixed with synthetic chemicals until he was nearly two but, trust me, there'll come a time when they get to a certain age and you won't be able to avoid it for much longer.

At about eighteen months it will be harder to ward off the pester power. They'll have seen the attraction of the sweet counter and the commercial lollies and sweeties their friends are eating, all brightly packaged and full of fun. However well you choose their friends, they'll be exposed to it and, almost as if they have antennae, they'll seek it out. At this point, you'll need to be creative and have a secret stash of your own carefully chosen sweets. Of course, it's as much about the packaging as the actual taste, but thankfully some suppliers are now cottoning on to this and providing relatively healthy treats in brightly coloured little packages. I know we're trying to do away with packaging, but try telling that to a toddler. At least with those tiny little boxes of organic raisins, you can reclaim the box after your child has finished, and reuse it putting in some more of your own organic raisins mixed with a few seeds.

For those times when nothing other than bought sweets will do, be prepared. Often the pressure can come from within your own family or from a caregiver. I lost count of the times I had to check whether one of my childminders was secretly giving my boys cheap, dodgy sweets – she actually thought I was being cruel not to allow them! Grandparents may well disagree with you over this issue and I know of several friends who have picked up their children after an afternoon with granny only to find them so hyper, they're crawling up the walls. 'Granny gave us a huge bag of sweets,' they brag. 'All the colours of the rainbow!'

Stand your ground; there will be many more years to come when what your child eats will not be your choice. Hold on to your power for as long as possible and don't back down. If your child is going to a childminder's or relative's house, send along the snacks you want him to have if you can't be sure that the ones provided will be suitable.

Fortunately, most health shops now offer some good alternatives to synthetic chemical sweets. For years I got away with giving my boys a little pack of Lafruit (little pieces of dried fruit that look like a bag of sweets). If your child is allergic to dairy you can get carob instead of chocolate. Carob raisins are very good as are the little carob chocolate buttons and Whizzers that look like little wrapped footballs. You can get them in most health food shops.

The best range I've found for making the kids really feel at one with their peers, particularly when they're a bit older, is Candy Tree. They do excellent wrapped, boiled sweet-type lollies, sweetened with corn syrup rather than sugar or synthetic sweeteners, and they contain no colouring. The brightly coloured wrapper does the trick. You can get these and a fantastic range of organic chocolate and sweet shop alternatives from the Organic Sweet Shop which also sells vegan, dairy- and gluten-free sweets (**www.stores.ebay.co.uk/The-Organic-Sweet-Shop**).

As I've mentioned, carob is a good alternative to chocolate, though, once they've tasted the real thing, there will be no going back. Most of the regular stuff and certainly the type branded for children is usually laden with sugar which can lead to all kinds of problems with blood sugar levels. Low cocoa solid chocolate often contains flavouring, fillers and additives. In addition, it contains caffeine, which is a stimulant. Bad idea! Go for organic chocolate, high in cocoa solids. If you get dark chocolate made with seventy to eighty per cent cocoa, after a couple of

squares, you feel quite satisfied and you'll end up eating less. For yourself (because after all, it's not only the kids that crave the stuff), the excellent news is the Women's Wonder Bar from Health by Chocolate (available at **www.lemonburst.co.uk**). This chocolate bar is an exclusive blend of soy, chaste berry and rose essential oil and delicious. Containing Omega 3, 6 and 9, it's perfect for premenstrual tension and for when you're feeling down. Guys will love it too. Divine chocolate and hot chocolate drink is hard to beat too. It's fair-traded and in most supermarkets.

Obviously, if your child has a wheat or gluten allergy you'll need to seek out specialist stuff but be careful, just because a commercially bought product is labelled wheat, gluten or dairy free, it doesn't mean it isn't high in sugar, artificial sweeteners, flavourings or hydrogenated fats. Look closely at the ingredients or get food made for you by a company such as **www.glutenfreebakery.co.uk**. There's always the option of using your bread maker for some sweet bread-style recipes.

## Sugar alternatives

What about sweeteners? What can you use to avoid the heaped teaspoonfuls over breakfast cereals? It's a good idea to avoid aspartame, saccharin, sucrose, sorbitol and all other hidden sugars at all costs but let's not forget that our bodies do need sugar to help with our energy levels. When our blood sugar levels drop, we can have a huge dip in energy. Conversely, if we give our bloodstream a huge sugar hit, it will create a more acid environment to compensate and all the other minerals and nutrients will be used up more quickly. That's when it's easy for little children, in particular, to be 'flying' one minute and sapped of energy the next. Their body starts to crave too much sugar which, if received, will reduce the amount of calcium in the bones. This also sets up a hugely difficult to break cycle of sugar highs and lows.

Once we start to crave sugar, complex carbohydrates such as grains and vegetables are the best option. It's worth remembering that if you roast carrots, peppers and sweet potatoes, it greatly increases their sweetness. If your children need an instant snack, offer them organic raisins or pieces of fruit.

There are a number of alternatives to sugar for sweetening food. Make some apple crisps (see page 131), powder them in a blender and sprinkle away.

Muscovado sugar is still sugar but it does contain the minerals and vitamins originally present in the sugar cane plant. You can also get organic raw cane sugar.

There's honey, of course, which is even sweeter than sugar, but at least it has natural sugars that help with digestion. If you can get local honey, it's also said to help with hay fever symptoms because you can build up your immunity to local pollens. If you can afford Manuka honey, this is antibacterial and antifungal, and it tastes fantastic. Most kids love it by the spoonful or spread on a finger of whole-meal toast. If your kids are not fans of honey, persevere. It's such a wonderfood and depending on the type you use, varies a lot in taste. Check out Rowse Speciality Honeys (**www.rowsehoney.co.uk**) for the finest range from around the world. They're available in the standard jars but also in squeezy bottles.

Molasses is thick and dark and very rich. It's so sweet that you need only the tiniest amount but it's a good alternative to treacle and it's great for baking. Organic maple syrup is perfect for drizzling over porridge or to use in flapjacks and date juice, to sweeten cakes or even as a drink.

A great alternative for drizzling, dolloping or cooking is Agave Nectar, which is an organic natural sweetener from The Groovy Food Company (which does great blends of omega 3, 6 and 9 oils). It is fructose extracted from the agave plant and has nothing added. It is suitable for diabetics, is gluten-free and is available from **www.groovyfood.co.uk** and in most supermarkets.

There is an ongoing debate about Stevia, which is said to be a great alternative to artificial sweeteners. Food authorities in the USA have been sceptical about it, however hence it's not allowed to be sold as a sweetener there, only as a nutritional supplement. It's been tried and tested successfully in Japan for forty years and in South America for hundreds of years. It's worth looking into if you're after a really natural alternative. You will need to get it imported into the UK. There's more information at **www.stevia.com**.

Xylitol is another sugar substitute that's widely available in supermarkets and health food shops under the brand name 'Perfect Sweet' (**www.perfectsweet.co.uk**). They claim it's a 100 per cent natural alternative to sugar. Sourced from corn and birch trees and said to be 'diabetic-safe', it won't interact with yeast so it can't be used for baking bread. (I use honey.) It can be used in hot drinks, on cereals and for baking.

My view is that all these substitutes continue to feed our sweet tooth habits and we should therefore attempt to lessen our craving for sugar. Just try cutting down, or even cutting it out. In my teens, I was a 'two spoonfuls in me tea' girl, but decided to give it up. Tea tasted disgusting! I held out though and, a year down the line, I was so used to no sugar that, when I accidentally picked up someone's sugar-laden cup and took a sip, it tasted so terrible I had to rinse my mouth out. It's all about attuning your tastes and, for our kids, keeping them healthier in the process.

# Snack treats

I've already pointed you in the direction of all my favourite, brilliantly comprehensive recipe books for the majority of the recipes you'll need for toddlers, but I thought it would be nice to include just a few very simple ones in case you can't find time to study a recipe book. These are the nutritional goodies that I have given my kids so they feel they are getting naughty treats. If you don't start down the route of commercially bought sugar and fat-laden goodies, you'll delay the fights a lot longer. Just make sure that you always have healthy snack options on offer.

## Fruit

Always have organic fruit available. A small piece of fruit, especially if it's lovingly cut up, will almost certainly do the trick for most toddlers. Buddy, at one, would always eat apple slices, but only if I'd cut them into 'rainbows'. Mangoes have absolutely taken over as the new King of Fruits in our house, a healthy option, treat and bribery tool all in one! (Make sure you slice and present them 'noughts and crosses' style.)

Dried fruit is good but do be a bit careful as it's very sweet. My boys went mad on fruit bars but didn't always remember to clean their teeth and I'm convinced that it contributed to the need for early dental work. If you do buy dried fruit, such as mango or apricot, buy the unsulphured variety and try to find organic (even though it's hideously expensive).

## Veggie sticks

Keep sticks of cucumber, red and yellow peppers and carrot in the fridge ready for the snack attack. You can also try offering a dip like humous or guacamole to liven them up.

If you need to use subterfuge, there are some nice ideas in The Art of Hiding Vegetables, Sneaky Ways to Feed Your Children Healthy Food by Karen Ball and Sally Child (White Ladder Press).

## Rice cakes

I'm a huge fan of rice cakes. The little bite size ones, in particular, are great for little children and you can also get flavoured ones. Corn cakes are an alternative – just look for the unsalted varieties. Oatcakes are great too, but be careful if your child has a gluten allergy and note that they can be quite salty. These can both be eaten on their own or spread with 100 per cent organic fruit spread, tahini, humous or Marmite. If your child is all right with wheat, breadsticks are good too. Baby Organix make some lovely baby bread-sticks that are perfect for little fingers.

## Popcorn

The other fab treat is a bag of popcorn.

Don't bother with a popcorn maker or a microwave, just buy the organic popping corn and pop away. All you need is a massive pan and a bit of oil. Obviously, get the unsweetened kind that makes a really healthy snack. A nice thing to do at children's parties is to give them all an A4 piece of brightly coloured paper to decorate with felt pens or stickers. Carefully fold the paper into a cone shape and secure with a small piece of tape, then fill with popcorn. It's just like being at the cinema – without the huge bucket of fizzy cola or the movie, but you could always put on a carefully chosen video.

## Make your own

For those of you who've got a bit of the domestic goddess in you, here are some ideas.

**Dried fruit** One way to avoid the sulphur dioxide in much of the commercially available dried fruit is to make your own. It works better with some fruits than others, but I have had good results with apples and bananas. Slice them and put them on a baking tray in the oven on a very low heat for a few hours. Add a sprinkle of cinnamon to the apples and nutmeg to the bananas.

**Crisps** When the dreaded cry for a bag of crisps goes up, slice pieces of potato, carrot, sweet potato, swede, beetroot and any other root vegetables as finely as possible and stick them under a very hot grill until golden and crispy. Let them cool and add a touch of salt. You can even make these with apples.

**Peanut butter boat** For a slightly more elaborate healthy treat, get a tiny piece of lettuce, fill it with peanut butter (I like Whole Earth) and add a stick of carrot or a baby sweetcorn as a sail.

Although I don't do cakes, I did manage to set my breadmaker to the mini muffin programme with fairly good results. I can also make most children's (and adults) parties rock with bowls of toasted nuts and seeds. Assuming your child doesn't have a nut allergy and is over a year old, try this:

### Toasted nuts and seeds
Take two handfuls of mixed nuts and seeds such as sesame, pumpkin, sunflower, cashew nuts, almonds, walnuts and pine nuts.

### Method
Heat a heavy based frying pan (no oil is needed) and when it's nice and hot, chuck in the nuts and fry till they're nice and golden, not burnt. For adults and older children, drizzle a few drops of Meridian Organic Tamari sauce over them, toss with a spatula. Turn out onto a ceramic plate and leave to cool before serving. To eat, just dig in – it's finger food at its best! (You can also sprinkle over salads and stir frys.)

### Nutty Biscuits
Obviously, this assumes that your child

doesn't have a nut allergy and I suggest them for age one or over.

Take a bowlful of mixed nuts and seeds such as sesame, pumpkin, sunflower, cashew nuts, almonds, walnuts, then grind them up, add a little filtered water until they're moist but not too wet, and form into biscuits. If you're feeling really creative you can use a cutter and make shapes like teddy bears or make faces with raisins for eyes. Bake them for about twenty minutes to half an hour and that's it.

Also healthy and easy are:

## Flapjacks
8 oz organic porridge oats
5 oz organic butter
1 tbs golden syrup
1 tbs Demerara sugar
2 oz ground almonds, ground flaxseeds, sunflower seeds, organic raisins.

### Method
Melt the butter and golden syrup (you can substitute molasses or agave nectar instead of treacle and coconut oil is healthier than butter) in a pan until the mixture starts to bubble. Stir in the oats. Adjust the recipe if the consistency doesn't seem right – it should be sticky but solid. Press into a baking tin and bake in an oven (gas mark 180) for about 12 minutes or until golden.

Add ground almonds, flaxseeds, sunflower seeds and a few raisins (up to 2 oz) to

make healthier. You could also try the Coco-Jacks from **www.coconoil.com**.

## Nutty balls
You may already know this recipe from Carol Vorderman's detox diet and she must take all the credit for this fab idea.

4 oz whole organic almonds
2 tbs Manuka honey (active 8+)
1–2 tsp filtered water
2–3 tsp ground cinnamon.

### Method
Grind the almonds in a coffee grinder until coarsely ground (not too fine – still with a few tiny bits). Knead with the honey and water in a mixing bowl until sticky but not too wet. Form into little balls, sprinkle cinnamon onto a chopping board and roll the balls until well coated. That's it – pop in mouth!

## Mini yoghurts
Most children love those little yoghurt pots that usually come branded with their favourite cartoon characters on the side. 'It's only fruit with yoghurt or fromage frais,' I hear you cry – 'that's healthy!' Sadly not, as most of them are loaded with added sugar, sweeteners and flavourings. Initially, you'll be able to get your baby to eat plain live organic yoghurt in any old bowl but once the 'I must have the mini versions' kicks in, you may need to buy them. Chuck the contents (or eat them yourself!) and sneakily fill the individual little pots with your own live

yoghurt mixed with puréed or well-mashed fresh raspberries or strawberries. I pride myself on this trick which has seen me through many a tantrum!

A fab healthy pudding is my:
## Summer fruit ice-cream surprise

Finely grind a small packet of cashew nuts and blend with a cup of organic rice milk to make a smooth paste. Add a tub of organic frozen raspberries (or any summer fruit) and blend. That's it! The surprise is that it becomes 'ice cream' because the fruit is frozen. If you leave it to melt, you have a gorgeous berry smoothie.

> As each day goes by, and with four children down the line, I can definitely say that fathering my children is the best thing I've ever done. And I won't be missing a minute of it.

**Imperfectly natural dad**

**Ice lollies** Come the hot weather, and particularly if there are older children around, there will come a time when you will face the issue of The Ice Lolly. Oh, one of life's great evils! If you count the colourings and flavourings in the average lolly, you really will be lolling your head. Just about all children are addicted to them. They're so cold and so sweet and, best of all, they can't really be shared and all toddlers hate sharing.

The solution? Make your own, of course. Get a good selection of those plastic, lolly-maker thingies from any supermarket or 'pound store' (I'm so sophisticated) and be creative. You can freeze any decent juice – but make it fresh juice, not from concentrate. Fresh apple, orange and mango all make great lollies. You can even purée your own fresh fruit and make one that way or add a bit of yoghurt for a creamy lolly. If you want to feel like a really perfect mother for five minutes, sneak in a bit of the juice that the vegetables are boiled in (not enough to taste). You could also sneak in some of the excellent oils from Viridian (**www. viridian-nutrition.com**).

A great way to make a really refreshing lolly is with some organic cordial. Rocks is a nice one (**www.rocksorganics.com**). Their ginger is really refreshing, as is elderflower for adults, but kids love the summer berries, and you can definitely sneak a bit of vegetable water in there! Be careful to keep the cordial in the fridge though and remember to check the 'use by' date, bearing in mind that when products aren't full of rubbish they don't keep so long. Try to find lolly makers with their own little lids and drill it into the kids that they must bring them back, or they'll get no more lollies. I know the ones with sticks seem easier but children will discard the sticks anywhere and everywhere and it's a devil of a job to replace them. Somehow a 'wonky' lolly just doesn't cut the mustard. You can freeze yoghurt and tofu-based fruit smoothies as 'popsicles' too.

**Drinks** Once your child is at the 'I must have a fizzy drink' stage, help is at hand from Whole Earth who, thankfully, make a great range of fizzy drinks in cans but without the caffeine and chemicals. You can get organic cola, lemonade and cranberry. For fresh juice, just make it yourself with any fruit and veg.

For a great treat, I love the Juice Master's chunk funky monkey from **7 lbs in 7 Days Super Juice Diet** by Jason Vale (Thorsons). It's chocolatey and banana-ish too. Just put the following ingredients in a blender and whizz until smooth:

1 banana
¼ tsp vanilla essence
1 tsp carob powder
250g live yoghurt or soya yoghurt
6 almonds
1 tsp Manuka honey
4 ice cubes

For those occasions when I've been just too imperfect to do anything other than open a carton, Ella's Kitchen Smoothie Fruits have proved to be a fantastic way of getting fruit into my toddler while he thinks he's getting an absolute treat. They're fab, 'toddler-sized' 100 per cent organic fruit smoothies, with nothing added and are available in most supermarkets or at **www.ellas kitchen.co.uk**.

# Food allergies

If your child has an allergy to something environmental then hopefully this book will help. If you think it's pollen, dust mites or pets then there are several ways to reduce the triggers. If it's a reaction to the chemicals in laundry detergents or cleaning products, there're lots of alternatives. Pinpointing food allergies can be more tricky.

Allergic reactions can result in symptoms such as excessive tiredness, irritable bowel, bloating, headaches, a runny nose or even a mild rash. Sometimes, it's not actually intolerance at all but the body not being able to process foods properly, perhaps because of a zinc deficiency for example.

Often there aren't any real symptoms. Children, even babies, can just seem out of balance. It's not as specific as being actually unwell, it may be difficulty sleeping, excessive crying, appearing sad or angry – all emotions and conditions that in a child are not unusual. Some allergic reactions, however, can even be life-threatening.

## Testing and treating allergies

When it comes to food, there are various allergy tests available, the most obvious of which can be simply to omit the suspect food from the diet for a period of time and see if symptoms improve. Wheat and dairy are good places to start.

Skin patch tests and blood tests can be arranged by a GP. A nutritional therapist is a better option in my view. To find a qualified nutritionist, dietician or nutritional therapist, go to.**www.bant. org.uk** or for those in private practice, go to **www.nutripeople.co.uk**.

Bio Resonance techniques are gaining in popularity. They include VEGA and MORA **www.en.wikipedia.org/wiki/ Bioresonance_therapy**. There's also NAET (Nambudripad's Allergy Elimination Techniques **www.naet.co.uk**), which are based on the theory that your own body has the unique ability to heal and rebalance itself if given the right messages. These techniques are designed to sort the problem to the extent that the body is reprogrammed to stop reacting to the allergen. Results can be spectacular or more subtle, and sometimes they may not work at all. It's good for babies, if

only for the fact that you're not putting drugs into your precious infant. Let's face it, there may be many more uncertainties about the effects of prescribed drugs than there are over the so-called scientifically unproven holistic methods of health treatment.

## Health kinesiology

This method takes a very holistic approach by almost asking the body what it needs. Gentle manipulation techniques are used to re-balance the body's energy systems. Treatment can also include the use of magnets, homeopathic remedies, flower essences, or even a particular thought. Health kinesiology has successfully treated arthritic pain, chronic fatigue, digestive problems, stress and tension, hormonal problems, skin conditions, menopausal symptoms and much more. It can also address phobias and worries and help you become more focused and increase your potential. Visit **www.hk4health.co.uk** for more information.

You must choose the kind of therapy that suits you best. I'd highly recommend health kinesiology for babies and children, particularly as it's incredibly gentle, quick (with my toddler who wasn't sleeping, it took one treatment) and effective and doesn't require, in most cases anyway, any avoidance period.

'Keep sticks of cucumber, red and yellow peppers and carrot in the fridge ready for the snack attack'

# Imperfectly naturally . . . unwell

'Let food be thy medicine and medicine be thy food.'
HIPPOCRATES

Obviously, I'm not a doctor and I can't give you the definitive guide to childhood illnesses or minor ailments here. All I'd like to do is show how the natural approach can be a blessing and point you in the direction of further help and remedies.

## Natural medicine cabinet

The most useful thing you can have in your kitchen is a medicine cabinet of natural remedies and the first thing to get is a good homeopathy kit. Kit from **www.ainsworths.com** or **www.helios.co.uk**. Speaking to a homeopath in person is very useful initially and it's always good to keep in touch with one in case things get complicated. Get a recommendation if you can, or the Alliance of Registered Homeopaths can put you in touch with one in your area (**www.a-r-h.org**). There is also information on **www.homeopathy-soh.org**.

Herbs are also wonderful in various forms such as tinctures, teas and creams. One organic and ethical supplier is **www.hambledonherbs.com**. To find a medical herbalist, try **www.nimh.org.uk**.

It's a good idea to keep some essential oils and a carrier, such as almond oil, for blending. Tea tree oil is antibacterial and antifungal, eucalyptus is great for colds and respiratory problems, and chamomile and peppermint are good for digestive upsets and relaxation. Remember not to take essential oils internally and never put them directly on an infant's skin. Of course, there can be contra-indications with aroma-therapy oils. Essential oils can be very potent, so make sure they're always well diluted, even for inhalation. You can also use a spoonful of milk to dilute essential oils. (For more information, visit **www.essentiallyoils.com** and **www.eoco.org.uk**.)

## Colic

Sadly, trapped wind affects many babies whether breast- or bottle-fed, and it's exhausting. It will pass, usually within three months, though I know that's no consolation if you're pacing the room at 2 a.m.

My first two boys both suffered from colic and, although I tried removing certain 'windy' foods from my diet and encouraged them to burp after feeding, it didn't really help. I found massage to be most beneficial but not while they were screaming! I'd try to pre-empt the most likely ocurrences by drinking chamomile or fennel tea. When they were having colic attacks, constant movement, talking to them and generally comforting them would often help.

Cranial osteopathy can help too and I also got my second baby a Bowen treatment that did seem to ease the colic considerably (see page 165). It's also worth trying the homeopathic remedy Colocynth 30. Just crush the tablet between two teaspoons and rub it gently along your baby's tongue or get it in granules from a pharmacy. You can also use Herbal Extract 'Windy-Pops'. It's organic, alcohol-free and formulated exclusively for children. You can buy it in health food shops and from **www.kinetic4health.co.uk**.

# Fever

It will be one of the most terrifying experiences of your life if your baby or infant develops a raging fever and, on this one, I must say, I find it extremely difficult to practise what I preach. Firstly, let's be clear and say that if your child develops a fever, you should consider consulting a doctor. If your newborn develops a fever, treat it as a potential emergency and seek help.

Now, let's look at the imperfectly natural approach alongside any conventional diagnosis and treatment. A fever is one of nature's own defence mechanisms and one of its best healing tools. When too much 'nonsense' accumulates in the body, and this can be mucus, synthetic chemicals from medication or bacterial infection, then the body's natural reaction is to rid itself of this waste before it causes serious problems. It's often at this point that the child will present with a cold, rash or other childhood illness such as chicken pox, mumps, scarlet fever or similar. The first sign of an impending illness is often the fever, which is the body trying to heal itself. What we ought to do, clearly, is allow the fever and aid it to cleanse the body and rebuild the very important white blood cells. Children can do this very quickly because they are so full of vitality.

Take your child's temperature (under the armpit is the safest place), and if it is high, keep your child hydrated. The body needs fluids and, if you're breastfeeding, by far the best thing is breast milk, totally on demand. Just 'hole up' and accept that your child needs to nurse for as long as he wants. Make sure you keep yourself hydrated too with plenty of water and perhaps some fennel tea to help boost your milk supply (see breastfeeding diet). If you're not breastfeeding, or in addition to milk, you can offer water at room temperature or diluted fresh juices. You can also offer a mild, warm herbal tea such as chamomile or ginger. Sweeten it with honey if your child prefers it that way. Don't worry about getting your child to eat. Look at animals, when they're unwell, instinctively they know it's time to fast.

It's a good idea to sponge the child down regularly but don't use freezing cold water, as this will just be a shock to the system. A good tip is to add a few spoonfuls of apple

cider vinegar to the water to maintain the pH balance of the skin. You can also get into a nice deep bath with your baby and add a cupful of ginger or chamomile tea. Sponge him down with cooler water and wrap him in wet towels or sheets if he still feels hot. Having said all this, I'm fairly sure that the first time this happens to you, you'll be sorely tempted simply to hot-foot it to casualty. Well, we're imperfect, aren't we, and it's better to be safe than sorry. If they send you home with medication, telling you to give it three times a day with lots of 'TLC', try a few hours of natural treatment first.

# Coughs and colds

I can't remember a winter for the last few years when my house hasn't sounded like a specialist chest hospital. I'm convinced both of my older boys had a version of whooping cough when they were three and four. It was thoroughly miserable and lasted the exact 100 days (whooping cough used to be called the 100 Day Cough).

These days most GPs very sensibly won't prescribe antibiotics if it's not an infection so, for viruses there really isn't any point in going down the medication route to alleviate symptoms. Most over-the-counter preparations for coughs and colds, even for children, contain a hair-raising number of synthetic chemicals that potentially could lead to more serious illness, rather than curing the mild one they used to alleviate. Take a look at that seemingly innocuous cough mixture and read in detail the ingredients and the list of possible side-effects that the manufacturers are obliged to warn you about. The good news is that there are lots of more natural ways to feel better. Most cough medicines don't usually even work, in my humble opinion.

Try to remember that a cold is the body's natural way of discharging all the junk it doesn't want, so try not to suppress the flow, messy though it might be. What you should be aiming to do is to assist the immune system to fight the cold. It's a good idea to give extra vitamin C and zinc for a few days. (A liquid version that is suitable for children under two is available from **www.biocare.co.uk**.) Also try Viridian, which has the largest organic supplement range, available in all good health shops and from **www.viridian-nutrition.com**.

If a child is suffering from congestion, the first priority is to keep him well hydrated. Give him water, diluted juice or, even better, old-fashioned lemon barley water made with pearl barley, organic lemons and organic sugar. Also run a hot bath or fill a basin with hot water. Add a few drops of lavender, olbas oil or antiseptic tea tree oil and inhale the steam, which helps to clear a stuffy nose. Alternatively, use a bowl and then make a kind of tent by putting the bowl on the floor, sitting on a chair and draping a blanket over a few chairs. Sit with the infant on your knee and breathe deeply. Children think it's just a fab game!

Honey and lemon with grated ginger is always a lovely warm drink and really does relieve a chesty cough or sore throat. Manuka honey is fantastically soothing and healing so try to get your child to eat it from a spoon. It's even more effective if you can crush a bit of garlic into it! Propolis tincture is also excellent for sore throats. If you just can't face making your own, for children over two, the Bryonia cough mixture from Ainsworths Homeopathic Pharmacy is excellent (**www.ainsworths.com**). They will also give you advice on homeopathic remedies for any ailment.

For sore throats, older children can gargle with lukewarm sage tea or a glass of water with a drop of tea tree added. This isn't really suitable for toddlers, as they'll just drink it. Apple vinegar and honey mixed together can be taken by the spoonful.

# Earache

This is a miserable affliction and I have just a couple of suggestions that may help. It's a good idea to try cutting out wheat and dairy for a few days. If your child has a temperature too, treat this as described on pages 140–43. What often works is a tiny drop of warmed olive oil poured gently into the ear. The other tip – and you're going to need to read this twice – is to hold a clove of garlic in the opening of the ear. Incredibly, garlic is antibacterial and antifungal and can work in the affected area in quite a short space of time. Children usually find it highly amusing. You could, of course, just use a drop of liquid garlic to do the same job. It's sensible to use a separate dropper for each ear so that you don't spread any infection. It's also soothing to massage gently around the ear with a drop of lavender oil or chamomile (in a carrier oil, of course).

If symptoms persist, see a doctor and if it is an ear infection and you have to give antibiotics, make sure you support the immune system with probiotics, which are available in powder or tablet form in any good health shop.

# Sticky eye and conjunctivitis

Always use clean cotton wool and water to bathe the eyes. Before using commercial ointments, if you're breastfeeding, try a little breast milk applied topically.

# Tummy upsets

Vomiting in children is quite common as their little digestive tract will just chuck food and drink back if it's not needed,

often leaving the child feeling almost instantly better. If the vomiting or diarrhoea is due to an infection though, the child may have a fever too. The most important thing is to keep your child hydrated, so offer water or a weak tea such as peppermint if you can get him to drink it. Continue to breastfeed too. A good homeopathic remedy that you can buy easily is Nux vom 30 (easy to remember) or Arsen alb 30. When your child starts to feel slightly better, give him non-allergenic, bland foods such as rice and pears.

For travel sickness (or morning sickness in you!), ginger will help. You can make a ginger tea by slicing it fresh from the root. Fennel tea will also help, or you can put a drop of lemon balm on a piece of cloth and inhale. For car journeys, I've had great success with the children's anti-sickness wristbands. They sit on acupressure points on the wrist and are available from chemists.

## Constipation

When constipated, babies won't want to eat much at all, but try to get your toddler to drink lots of water and fresh vegetable juices. Try mixing them with fresh fruit juice if you need to make them more palatable. Try giving dried apricots as snacks, and giving a soothing tummy massage.

## Pains and bruises

For general aches and pains, bathe in Himalayan salt or Epsom salts. Make a compress with lavender or rosemary oil. Or use an ice pack for nasty sprains. For bruising, take arnica tablets and rub on arnica cream. A vinegar or witch hazel compress can also help. For mild knocks and bumps, take Rescue Remedy for the shock as well as arnica tablets and then apply arnica cream (but not if the surface is cut). Calendula and hypercal are also excellent for bruises and wounds. If you can get it, comfrey cream is also good for bruising and swelling.

For headaches, gently massage peppermint or lavender oil around the temples or use a Tiger Balm rub. Living Nature (**www. livingnature.co.uk**) make a petroleum-free natural one.

## Cuts and wounds

Manuka honey (available from **www. naturesnectar.co.uk**) is a wonder food that also works as an antibacterial healer when applied to cuts and wounds. It's even being used in hospitals now. Hypercal cream is excellent for cuts and grazes.

## Skin problems

For itchy skin, sit in a lukewarm bath and run the water through a muslin bag or an old stocking filled with oats (see pages 52–4).

Helichrysum hydrosol is fantastic for rashes. It's anti-inflammatory, analgesic and reduces swelling and bruising. You can even use it as a mouthwash for receding gums (not the baby's, yours!) It's contained in 'Instant Relief', a gentle spray that helps with any inflamed rashes or itchy bits (available from **www.sensitiveskincareco.com**).

Neem tree products made in India to Ayurvedic recipes also help with psoriasis and dry skin. Look at **www.neemtree.info**.

## Bites and stings

If you can't find a dock leaf, try rubbing lavender oil on a nettle sting. For wasp stings, use vinegar or lemon juice and for bee stings, bicarbonate of soda will ease the pain (make a paste with a little water). For mosquito bites, use tea tree oil and aloe vera gel straight from the plant. Immediately after being bitten, take the homeopathic remedy Apis.

To repel insects, use the excellent Badger Balm 'anti-bug' balm, which is available in supermarkets. There are now also several natural 'bug repellent' sprays and a spray you can use on your clothes – Health Guard from **www.avea.co.uk**.

## Sore lips

For chapped and sore lips, avoid the petroleum-based products and try a natural lip balm. Go to **www.naturally tejas.com** and **www.spiezia organics. com**.

## Burns and scalds

For serious burns, seek help immediately. For minor burns, apply neat lavender oil, unless the burn is on a very young child, in which case you should dilute it with a carrier oil such as olive oil. If you have an aloe vera plant, snip it and use the gel. The other thing that sounds daft but helps is a cold tea bag (preferably chamomile) held against the scalded area. Once the burn starts to heal, use hypericum tincture. For blisters, soak the area in water with some Himalayan salt added and when dry apply witch hazel.

## Sunburn

For sun protection, do not just slap on any old sun cream as these are potentially full of toxic chemicals that could do your infant's skin more harm than a dose of sunshine.

Firstly, I shout from the hilltops – cover up! Kit out your babies and toddlers in sun hats. These are easier to keep on babies

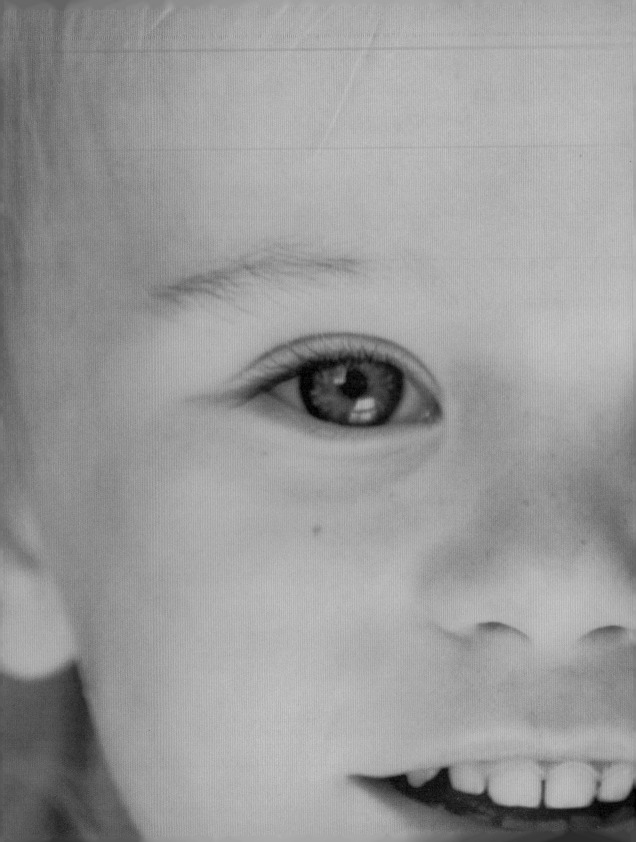

than toddlers, I know, but be prepared to use bribery. Try **www.sun-togs.co.uk** for great protective clothing. Use a 'natural' sunscreen such as the organic sun cream for babies from Green People (**www.greenpeople.co.uk**). (For you, by the way, they also make a more natural fake tan.)

Zinc oxide is the most effective form of sunblock and surfers have got it right with their white noses. We can now emulate that a bit with Caribbean Blue, a sunblock that contains zinc oxide in a transparent form. It is available from **www.olive organic.co.uk**.

If you're unfortunate enough to get really sunburnt, both lavender oil and coconut oil are very soothing.

If it's a case of sunstroke, try the homeopathic remedy Belladonna, which will bring down the temperature and relieve the headache.

## Teething and toothache

For teething pain, I'd recommend the homeopathic remedy Chamomilla 30, crushed and rubbed along the gums. This is safe even for babies. You can also try a bit of Rescue Remedy along the gums too. For older kids and adults, a drop of clove oil on the tooth really helps until you can get to the dentist.

## Head lice

It makes you shudder just to think about it! My first two boys got to the ripe old age of six and seven before they got nits but, sure as eggs is eggs, they got them eventually. Head lice 'knit' themselves to the hair and are a devil to get out. Usually, they re-infest at **www.nits.net**. Get their 'bug busting' combs (even available on prescription) and use a magnifying glass unless your eyesight is airline pilot fantastic. Follow their instructions for 'de-lousing' at intervals over a two-week period.

There are special shampoos available, but I would avoid them like the plague. Most contain toxic chemicals that even nits don't deserve. Fortunately, you can now get Biz Niz shampoo and leave-in conditioner, which are free of parabens and 'nasties', in health food shops and chemists. As a preventative measure, use tea tree oil and lavender oil around the nape of the neck or put some on a hairbrush and comb it through the hair at night.

To be on the safe side, wash bed linen and towels regularly and, if you co-sleep, be aware that the little horrors could be jumping from your child's scalp to yours. (I'm itching just writing this!)

## More information

For an 'at a glance' reference chart for mild

## Natural First Aid Remedies

This is an at-a-glance reference chart for mild conditions only – for serious or persistent symptoms – seek qualified medical advice.

| | |
|---|---|
| **Aches & Pains** | Lavender, rosemary & marjoram compress. Epsom Salts in bath. Tiger Balm rub (in tubes). Rheumatism/joint cold – Arnica cream (in tubes). |
| **Bites & Stings** | Wasps: Vinegar or lemon juice. Bees: Bicarbonate of soda (make a "bee" sting wet applied – can leave in water ©). Mosquito: Tea-tree oil, aloe-vera. Nettle: Dock-Leaves, lavender |
| **Blisters** | Witch-hazel. Lavender oil. Salt water. Aloe-vera. Calendula. Rescue Remedy |
| **Bruises** | Arnica (arm or cream). Cold Packs. Witch hazel. Vinegar compress. Wet Cabbage Leaves |
| **Burns and Scalds (mild)** | IMMEDIATELY: Hold area under cold water for at least 10 minutes. (For minor burns & scalds only). Aloe vera (fresh leaf or gel). Lavender oil (in water & bathe). Calendula & hypericum tincture. Cold wet tea-bag (on scalds) |
| **Colds** | Coughs: Radish tea, Lemon & honey. Congestion: Inhalation of: tea-tree, eucalyptus, olbas oil. + ensure good regular supply of Zinc & Vitamin C in diet |
| **Cuts & Abrasions** | Calendula & hypericum cream. Lavender oil. Tea-tree oil (dilute). Aloe vera (skin wash). Salt Water ©. Honey. |
| **Earache** | Warm olive oil (suggest into ear). Mullein or St.John's wort oil (in ear). Lavender & chamomile oil. Sometimes better with HEAT. IF IMPORTANT PERSIST – SEE A DOCTOR |
| **Headaches** | Infusions of: Fever-tea, Meadowsweet, Valerian, Vervain, ginger. Peppermint & Lavender oils (rub on temples) |
| **Head lice** | Oils of: Citronella, Lavender, Eucalyptus, Geranium, rosemary. Comb wet hair & apply & leave on overnight comb out – repeat & interval |
| **Mouth Ulcers** | (Rock Salt adequate strong & remedy) Ginger Root – chew it. Myrrh oil or tincture. Aloe vera (rinse). Geranium oil ©. Lavender oil (freshwater) |
| **Nausea** | (Try valerian or lemon balm for anxiety) Travel Sickness : ginger capsules as in rock). Peppermint tea. Lavender oil – in sniff. Indigestion: Fennel, peppermint, Lavender, chamomile teas |
| **Shocks & knocks (mild)** | Rescue Remedy™. Arnica (tablets & cream). Lavender oil rub. Chamomile Tea |
| **Sleeplessness** | Warm baths. Lavender oil. Chamomile Tea. Valerian, Vervain & Lemon balm teas |
| **Sore Skin** | Sore skin: aloe vera, calendula cream. Baby skin: chickweed (lowers) add to a bath). Sunburn: aloe vera, cold tea (on skin) Lavender oil. |
| **Sore Throat** | Thyme inhalation. Sage tea gargle. Warm salt water gargle. Tea-tree oil gargle (dilute in warm water). Apple vinegar & honey. Lavender oil massage (around neck) |
| **Toothache** | Clove or peppermint oil (on tooth). Garlic clove on tooth. ABSCESS: comfrey or myrrh tincture mouthwash. Chew sage-leaves or garlic |
| **Verrucas & Warts** | Banana skin – put the inside against the wart, plaster on, over night. Tea-tree oil, garlic, fresh Lemon juice. |

For orders contact Lemonburst, UK 01225 (no.) www.lemonburst.net

conditions, get yourself the beautifully designed 'Natural First Aid Remedies' chart (see left) from **www.lemon burst.co.uk**.

I would recommend The Complete Homeopathy Handbook by Miranda Castro. She has also written Mother and Baby (Miranda Castro's Homeopathic Guides).

The best book I've found with an A to Z of natural remedies for everyday children's ailments is What Really Works for Kids by Susan Clark (Bantam Press).

# Flower essences

I'm a very big fan of Bach Flower Rescue Remedy and go nowhere without it. There are still a huge number of sceptics who say it's merely the minute drop of alcohol used as a preservative that helps you through the crisis but, as with so many things, I don't care too much how it works, only that it does for me.

Last year I came across a fantastic new range of essences for babies and children. A kind of 'first aid kit for feelings' to help with emotional bumps and

bruises, this series of essences is called Indigo Essences (**www.indigoessences. com**). They are described as a 'sort of vibrational medicine which contains the healing pattern of a flower or a stone'. Even very young children can choose their own essences and seem intuitively to know exactly what they need. I'd also recommend the 'Elixirs for Life' range of flower and gem essences from **www.tortuerouge.co.uk**. See also **www.speciallittlepeople.co.uk**.

# To vaccinate or not to vaccinate?

If you've flicked straight to this page expecting to read how to go about getting separate vaccinations instead of MMR, you may well be disappointed. This topic is so huge and so emotive, it would require another hefty book to do it justice.

My best advice is this – whether this is your first or subsequent baby, be informed. Remember, vaccinations are not compulsory in the UK. Don't simply 'tow the line' when it comes to routine immunisation, unless you have thoroughly researched both sides of the argument and discussed the consequences with your co-parent. For all the pro-vaccination information you'll find out there, there's just as much anti-vaccination data, not all compiled by 'quacks' as the official line might have you believe. Also, you may find

it enlightening to seek out the wealth of anecdotal evidence from families and parents. I find it incredible that this is mostly ignored by many in the scientific community.

If you have an appointment card dropped through the door for your child's MMR, you don't have to cancel it forever. Postpone it until you can go into the surgery with no fears or qualms, because you personally are basing your decision not on any official guidelines or while under any pressure, but because you are informed and comfortable with your decision.

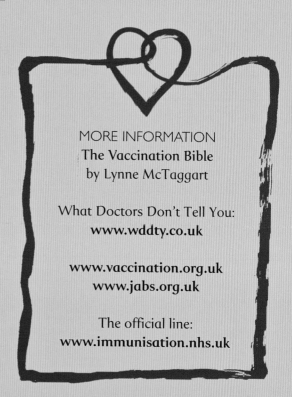

MORE INFORMATION
The Vaccination Bible
by Lynne McTaggart

What Doctors Don't Tell You:
**www.wddty.co.uk**

**www.vaccination.org.uk**
**www.jabs.org.uk**

The official line:
**www.immunisation.nhs.uk**

# Looking after yourself

'A mother's children are portraits of herself.'
UNKNOWN

There's no doubt that the way you look after yourself will affect your children. Your powders and potions, along with your sense of wellbeing will, literally, rub off on them so, if you haven't thought about it before, now is the time to aim at being an imperfectly natural parent.

# Skin and hair care

Not surprisingly, the terrifying collection of chemicals used in the manufacture of baby toiletries (see pages 54–6) is also in your products. So, when the time comes to indulge in some pampering, choose your products wisely.

Starting with sunscreen, don't buy into the 'every moisturiser must have a Sun Protection Factor' thing; cover up with a huge hat and shades and use only natural sunscreen. Also, accept that giving birth may cause changes in your skin. It's common for moles to appear during pregnancy so, if you're at all concerned, I highly recommend a full-body screening (visit **www.themoleclinic.com**).

I would take the purist approach and start from the premise that you shouldn't put anything on your skin that you wouldn't want to eat. I therefore recommend two natural wonders that are pure enough to be eaten as well as absorbed into the skin.

Coconut oil is the cheapest, best and most wonderful moisturiser you will ever find. It's great for stretch marks and for babies, it's excellent for massage as well as cradle

cap. There are lots of makes around but my favourite is still Coconoil from Sri Lanka (available from **www.coco noil.com**).

Himalayan salt can be used as regular salt but it's also great to put in the bath. It is rich in calcium, magnesium, potassium, copper and iron, which gives the salt its beautiful pink colour. It can help the body detox and soothe muscular pain. Salt also helps with healing after an episiotomy. Go to **www.saltshack.co.uk** and **www.kudos rocksalt.co.uk**.

## A word about soap and water

The problem with regular soap is that it is incredibly drying and, among other things, can contain lanolin and sodium lauryl sulphate, a surfactant found in many skincare ranges that can cause skin irritation.

Some soaps, cleansers and body lotions also contain petrolatum or mineral oil, both petrochemical products. Imidazo-lidinyl urea, DMDM hydantoin and methyl, propyl, butyl and ethyl paraben are preservatives and sensitisers that are thought to contribute to allergic reactions

and even cancers. There are too many great natural soaps to list here but check out Essential Spirit handmade soaps (**www.essentialspirit.co.uk** ). The palm oil used in their soap is certified organic and I've managed to convert the whole family to their Organic Hemp soap. Liquid soaps that are 100 per cent organic are available from **www.ecosoapia.com**.

## Facial cleansers and moisturisers

You'll need to have a good look at what's around in this area and discern your favourites based on your skin type. The important thing is to avoid synthetic perfumes, parabens and petrochemicals.

I've recently treated myself to the Age Reverse face cream by Eva (**www.eva-cosmetics.de**), which contains the rare Argan oil, said to be very healing and protective against damaging effects of the sun. It's one of the few totally organic ranges that can be bought in selected department stores. There are many excellent natural skincare products available. Just look at the choice on offer from **www.sensitiveskincareco.com**, **www.nealsyardremedies.com**, **www.aubreyorganics.com**, **www.summer naturals.co.uk**, **www.purelyfor you.co.uk**, and **www.oliveorganic.co.uk**.

For base oils and creams and excellent quality essential oils, check out **www.essentiallyoils.com** and for essential

oils and lots of associated products, try The Essential Oil Company (**www.eoco.org.uk**). You can also get all-natural perfumes from **www.avea.co.uk** and **www.lemonburst.co.uk**.

## Cosmetics

I'm pleased to say that, finally, I've replaced nearly everything in my make-up bag with a synthetic-free, chemical-free, organic alternative. I now use bits and bobs from many different ranges. Have a really good look and see what suits you best. I love the liquid foundation from Living Nature (**www.livingnature.co.uk**) and the concealer from the Miessence range (**www.sheer organics.com** or **www.totallyorganics.co.uk**).

I use lipsticks, lip glosses, eye shadows and eyeliner pencils from Sante at **www.avea.co.uk** and some gorgeous mineral powder blushers and translucent powders from Lily Lolo (**www.lilylolo.co.uk**).

## Deodorants

If you want to start somewhere on this natural path, start with replacing your deodorant. Most regular deodorants contain a whole bunch of perfumes, parabens, alcohol and petrochemicals along with other unnecessary gubbins, not to mention aluminium, which really should not be placed in that very sensitive area. Ditch them all and go for a natural

deodorant, such as the one that comes from **www.crystal deodorant.com** in a cute little bamboo carrying case. You can try one out for under £2 with the travel-size Crystal Deodorant from **www.lemon burst.co.uk** and health shops.

Another really unusual alternative that I'm trying as we go to print is the Amazing Body Stick. It's simply a high-grade stainless steel disk. When it comes into contact with water or odour, the pongy molecules are destroyed at source. You just rub it around your armpit for twenty or thirty seconds and it will neutralise any odours. The manufacturers say it will never wear out, so it lasts a lifetime – not bad for £19.95 (visit **www.thenaturalcollection. com**.) I'm now wondering whether rubbing the top of my stainless steel flask around my armpit will do the same job. Could be worth a try!

TOP
IMPERFECTLY
NATURAL TIP

Rub the juicy side of
a lemon around your armpit
– it makes a fantastic
anti-perspirant!

## Shampoo

It won't surprise you to know that most shampoos are full of sodium lauryl sulphate, perfumes, parabens and petrochemicals. Usually, the brighter the colour, the worse they are! You can, however, buy shampoos with staggeringly few ingredients, often from small companies run by women who have sourced their own perfect shampoo ingredients and hit upon a winning natural formula. Have a look at **www.hemp garden.co.uk**, **www.sensitiveskin careco.com** and **www.avea.co.uk**.

## Soapnuts

These little sustainable wonders really do make fantastic shampoo as well as being brilliant for the washing. All you need do is boil six or seven soapnut shells in water and simmer for about twenty minutes. The mixture won't look great, just like brown water really, but if you whisk it up into a foam, you have a lovely shampoo. It leaves your hair gloriously shiny and silky and costs very little. (See pages 48-9 for more information on soapnuts and suppliers.)

## Conditioners

Conditioning is something else that most hair types need, and most of the companies selling natural shampoos also offer a chemical-free conditioner. However, it is easy to make your own rinses and conditioners. My favourite, coconut oil, makes an excellent deep conditioner for dry and damaged hair but you will need to rinse your hair really well. You can also make your own rich conditioner for dry hair with half a ripe avocado and 5 ml of avocado oil or olive oil. Add one egg yolk and mash it all into a paste. Homemade mayonnaise is brilliant too.

For psoriasis, try some Neem oil if you can get hold of it. It's antifungal and antiseptic. Rosemary is a fantastic essential oil to use or, better still, get a few sprigs of fresh rosemary, steep them in water, strain and use the liquid as a final rinse. A few drops of lavender and sandalwood oil added to water is excellent for dealing with dandruff. Lemon juice is good as a final rinse, especially for blonde hair, as it has a gentle lightening effect.

Of course, healthy hair starts from within, as does just about everything. Look at what you're eating. I may sound like a stuck record but a diet of organic fruit and vegetables is so important. You'll need Omega 3 and 6 (see Good Food for Mother and Baby, page 106). Wild seaweed is a good supplement for luscious, shiny hair too.

## Hair colour

Be wary of regular hair dyes (see my first book) and be especially careful not to begin dyeing dark hair in pregnancy as some of the ingredients can cause severe allergic reactions. For alternatives, one of the purest 'do it yourself' herbal hair colour ranges is from Logona (**www.logona. co.uk**). My blonde highlights are done at Daniel Fields Organic and Mineral Hairdressing Salon in Herts. Also see **www.organiccoloursystems.com**.

# Hands and nails

## Hands

We all know our hands show our age and, although we can't halt the ageing process, we should look them – after all, we expect them to do an awful lot for us. Start with the massage and moisturising bit. Pamper yourself with a hand mask or exfoliating scrub. Then file your nails using a glass nail file and keep them well oiled with sweet almond or olive oil.

Many hand creams contain lanolin and various petrochemical substances. Avoid these by trying some of the lovely, rich hand creams that are now available with organic or mineral ingredients, and without parabens, sodium lauryl sulphate and other nasties. A great way of keeping your hands looking good is to have a hand massage – either go to a salon or do it yourself. Work oil or cream around your hands and wrists, then concentrate on the fingers one at a time. An excellent exfoliating scrub is fine

Himalayan or sea salt or lemon juice (not if you have any cuts around the nails though) mixed with olive or coconut oil. Add scent with one drop of an essential oil such as rose or lavender. You can do exactly the same for your feet with a drop of peppermint oil, which is really invigorating.

## Nails

I'm thrilled to announce the glorious news that there are now some less toxic and more environmentally friendly nail polishes available. These include Suncoat (**www.suncoateurope.com**), a water-based nail polish. All the chemical solvents have been replaced by water and it's naturally coloured with earth pigments. No synthetic dyes are used and there are over forty colours in the range, from natural through pinks, reds and even bright metallic blue.

Sante (**www.santecosmetics.co.uk**) sells acetate-free nail-varnish remover with organic orange oil, nail fluid pens and a range of twenty-six shades of nail polish that are free from formaldehyde, rosins, toluene, colour lakes and phthultes. I've found that these non-toxic polishes dry quicker than regular ones and do last a good week without chipping. If you can get to a salon for a pampering, get a natural manicure from **www.greenhands.co.uk**.

Now you've finished pampering yourself, you're about as imperfectly natural as you can get. In the exploration process you'll find many new brands that will become your favourites, so let me know about the ones you love (on **www.imperfectly natural.com**) and I'll spread the word.

# Feminine care

Once you start having periods again it will come as quite a shock. Other than the lochia after the birth, you may have had almost a year and half without menstrual bleeding. Apart from everything else, you now have to consider sanitary protection too.

This is one area where a small change really does make a big difference to your purse, the environment and your health. My recommendation is to ditch the usual disposable tampons or towels. They are terrible for the environment, expensive and often bleached and coated in some possibly toxic, synthetic chemicals that you don't want in contact with that very sensitive area. The best advice is to use washable pads or invest in a menstrual cup. Since using mine, my blood flow has been lighter and my menstrual cramps have reduced. This could be as a result of avoiding the chemicals in tampons, which dry out the vaginal area and cause cramping. The best-known product is the Mooncup (**www.mooncup.co.uk**) and it will last you a good ten years. For menstrual pain, try the Ladycare Magnet

# Imperfectly natural parent

**Your name, age group, age of children** Mary Henn 39, children Felix, 6, Archie, 4, and Lily, 1.

**Occupation?** Building surveyor specialising in historic buildings working for the National Trust. I'm now a self-employed building surveyor and operations manager for the Dutch Nursery Garden Centre.

**Birth experiences – natural/assisted?** Supposedly natural! With my first baby, I had 18 hours on my back with excruciating pain so had mobile epidural – strapped to monitor with no explanation for four hours, and then found it too painful to move around so delivered on my back on bed. My cut was stitched up like the Bayeux Tapestry and then had a haemorrhage. With Archie, more of the same. Not quite so painful, so had gas and air for eight hours. Placenta delivered with the help of drugs so no haemorrhage but tore and had lots of stitches. He had cord round his neck several times so had to be brought back to a pink colour from blue. For Lily, I did lots of preparation with Dr Gowri Motha so it was quick – start to finish in under four hours. Very painful but didn't have any drugs and I could focus through the pain and concentrate on the result.

**Your emotional state for the first six months?** Had post-natal depression after both Felix and Archie. Was a mess with Felix, with Archie it was slightly better. With Lily, apart from a couple of low days, absolutely fine.

**Your physical health?** After Felix and Archie, I was shot to pieces – took ages to recover. With Lily, it took a week to feel a little more human.

**When did your figure return? Did you exercise?** I am still waiting! Exercise – Felix six months after, Archie a year and Lily within about three months (Pilates).

**How was your relationship with your partner?** Very bad after Felix and Archie. Okay after Lily but primarily because I felt all right and I had help which I didn't have after first two. My husband didn't understand post-natal depression and how debilitating it is.

**Breastfeeding experience?** Got off to bad start with Felix – he would not latch on, took all the skin off my nipples and I had to hire an industrial breast pump. I persevered for three months but it was totally unenjoyable. Archie was a much better feeder from day one and I managed to feed him for six months. With Lily it was fine and I carried on for a year.

**Nappies – if cloth, which type do your prefer and why?** At birth used Imsy organic cotton terry nappies. For convenience, I use some Motherease all-in-ones. Until they make disposables that are biodegradable, I won't use them.

**What's in your medicine cupboard for the children?** Tea tree oil, lavender, arnica, arnica cream. Nurofen and Medised only used in desperation when nothing else will work and the child is in terrible pain.

**What do you do to keep 'sane'? What do you do for 'me' time?** I am not sane! I don't have much 'me' time at the moment. When I do, I like to curl up somewhere outside and read a very low-brow magazine or listen to the Archers, which for some reason I find very reassuring.

**Sleep (or lack of)?** I need about eight hours a night but at the moment I can't sleep properly. I don't go to bed early enough and feel like I am half awake all night – I feel exhausted.

**Sex (or lack of)?** No complaints – not very often but I am too knackered to care!

**Skincare – soaps, moisturisers, sunscreen?** I try to use natural products wherever possible. I very rarely use anything at all on the children – just water. The less stuff I put in the bath, the better, as I am siphoning it out and using it on the garden – trying to use gadgets to do so: www.droughtbuster. co.uk and www.banbeater.co.uk.

**How do you deal with challenging behaviour?** If I am feeling okay, I try to ignore it to start with and then reason with the children – Archie is too young to understand reason though. If I am knackered or upset I find it very difficult to keep my calm and far too often end up shouting and screaming, which I know I shouldn't do and has absolutely no effect.

**What do you hear yourself saying to your children often that you wish you didn't?** 'When I was a child I was made to eat everything!' 'Some children don't have any toys!' 'If you do that again I'll…'

**As a family, how green are you? 10 is dark and leafy, 1 is a faint hint of peppermint.** I would say 5.

**Do you recycle everything?** We recycle 90 per cent of everything – but let down by my husband emptying the recycling bins into the dustbins on the odd occasion.

**Do you consider fair-trade/ethical trading?** Yes – I am particularly keen on buying organic cotton whenever possible. It is always a consideration every time I make a major purchase. I will also buy fair-trade groceries whenever it is an option. I only buy timber and timber products which are FSC-approved (Forestry Stewardship Council) and will only buy British lumpwood charcoal.

**What's your top ten eco-family tip?** Try to reduce the amount you buy in the first place. Get the children involved in recycling.

**At what age do you think 'screens' are okay?** Felix desperately wants a PlayStation but I won't let him have one – too expensive anyway. I let them watch TV for about an hour a day.

**Your top three tips for imperfectly natural parenting?** Relax – let them run around outside, get filthy dirty and get a few cuts and grazes. Don't make food into an issue – let them eat the odd bit of junk food, then eat rice and veg on another day. If they won't eat their lunch, just take it away, they will eat when they are hungry. Make sure they know you love them regardless of how vile they are being.

**Parenting pleasures – what do you most love about being a mum? What are your imperfections?** I love being part of their journey of discovery – finding out how things work and what they can do – first steps, first words, first tennis match. I love their affection – which I get some of the time.

**Do you keep all the balls in the air? If not, why not? Is it lack of time?** Yes, I do try, but they keep falling down and hitting me the face. I try to be everything to everyone – setting myself up for failure. I should just accept that you can't do everything perfectly, so you either have to drop your standards sometimes or try to do fewer things at once.

**Anything else you'd like to share to help towards an imperfectly natural world?** As one person, you can only do so much. Stick to what you believe in and find reasons for doing things, not reasons for not doing things. Don't analyse things too much – you can only make decisions based on the information you have at the time. If you make the wrong decision, learn from it and don't beat yourself up about it.

which is a tiny magnet that sits in your knickers. It's available in good pharmacies or at **www.ladycare health.com**. For lots more information, see my first book.

## Keeping fit

Hopefully, since you ventured out from your babymoon period and completed your post-natal exercises (vital to help reposition the uterus), you've been walking as much as possible, with your baby in a buggy or a sling. Walking is a fantastic way of exercising and lifting your spirits, plus saving money and fuel at the same time. If you're really keen, get a three-wheeler buggy and jog, but even a brisk walk around a local park will do the trick.

If you read my first book, you'll know that I highly recommend bouncing for all-round fitness. Get yourself a good rebounder (mini-trampoline) and bounce away; the kids will love it too. Try the Pro-bounce from **www.juicemaster.com**.

Swimming is great for getting back into shape after the birth. Some pools even offer swimming courses for babies and it's a great idea to get them used to splashing around as early as possible. If you can, find one that's ozone-treated rather than chlorinated.

Check out your local library, as often they'll have details of classes in the area.

You can now go to buggy fitness classes too. I think the idea is that you push the buggy around to music.

Yoga is, of course, one of the best forms of exercise to build up your strength and stamina and there are various places now running baby yoga classes that mother and baby can do together.

If you're as imperfectly lazy as I am, you'll also want to know about the 'passive exerciser', the Chi Machine (**www.chi-machine.co.uk**). Some therapists use it in combination with the most amazing plug-in healer, the Far Infra-red (FIR) Hothouse. This is a medically patented device that originates from Japan (beware cheap imitations with the wrong wave-length). You just lie under the gentle heat and feel it restoring your energy. It's said to enhance immunity, aid detoxification, help reduce cellulite, rebalance hormones, dramatically improve skin and increase energy, while promoting deep relaxation. It is available at discount rates from Sue at **www.integralnutrition.co.uk**.

## Therapies

Sadly, I do not have the space in this book to go into all the different healing treatments that are available, so I have picked out a few of my favourites that I believe are incredibly beneficial post-birth, or for those times when your children are young and you feel particularly frazzled.

If you are thinking of giving yourself a treat, the most important thing to remember is that you really should find a good, recommended therapist. Personally, I have had some terrible treatments where the practitioner has just gone through the motions. Quite possibly, the certificates on the salon wall were entirely 'kosher', but not everyone who has qualified has 'healing hands'. I've had aromatherapy massages where the oil is chosen just because it's open and I've lain there feeling like a piece of meat being perfumed on a slab. Fortunately, I now know that if I can't have a trial session (look out for local 'indulgence evenings' where you can have a taster treatment for about £5), I will need to go to an accredited body to find someone who is not just qualified but rated as holistic. The Federation of Holistic Therapists (**www.fht.org.uk**) makes sure their practitioners have achieved the highest level of accredited training.

Another organisation well worth joining is The Wellbeing Network (**www.well beingnetwork.co.uk**), an online community where you can access the best products, services and skills related to wellbeing. The work of their accredited therapist members is reviewed and has to attain certain criteria before they can be recommended. All of these therapies are covered in more detail in my previous book Imperfectly Natural Woman.

## Light therapy

If you feel down during the winter months or simply don't get enough daylight, consider a light box designed to help sufferers of Seasonal Affective Disorder (SAD). Just switch on the lamp while you potter around. It's great for fractious children on dark winter afternoons as it gives them the energy to keep going until bedtime. Visit **www.wholistic research.com** and **www.sad.uk.com** or **www.litebook.com** (for portable lights).

## Magnetic therapy

I talk a lot about magnetic therapy and my enthusiasm for it has not waned. I'm convinced wearing my Bioflow bracelet made labour much less painful. The theory is that the magnetic bracelets made by Ecoflow (**www.ecoflow.plc.uk**) use a unique central reverse polarity system that stimulates the blood flow. They work for a multitude of ailments and, I believe, preventively. (Incidentally, they also work brilliantly on injured animals, where there can be no placebo effect!) For pain relief using magnets, contact Changing Lives 01736 799519 or **www.changinglives-stives.co.uk**.

## Massage

Bear in mind that it is especially important to be touched and have your skin's elasticity and muscle tone restored after labour (see page 18).

Even if you can't afford a professional therapist, it's worth trying to get the baby looked after for half an hour every day while your partner gives you an aroma-therapy massage. Hopefully, you will have got him trained during pregnancy so he'll have the knack, but it doesn't have to be an exact science. It's just an opportunity for you to lie still and relax in a warm room, perhaps with a lighted candle. Mix aromatherapy oil – rose otto is very uplifting – in some carrier oil, and get your partner to make firm sweeping movements across your back, neck, shoulders and legs. It will really help to restore your skin tone and relieve your aching muscles. If you're tired, it will revive you. (See pages 60–62 for more on baby massage.)

## Cranial osteopathy

One of the most wonderful healing treatments you can have for both you and your baby, as soon as possible after birth, is cranial osteopathy. It's a form of osteopathy that works specifically on the skull. It's an extremely gentle manipulation of the face and head and is effective both during pregnancy and after a difficult labour. There is also craniosacral therapy, a light touch technique based on cranial osteopathy that aims to restore the natural rhythm that flows through the core of the body. It helps to clear blockages in the sacrum and the bones of the skull and releases emotional stress and traumas, the memory of which is stored within the body,

possibly affecting the health and wellbeing of the patient.

The theory is that the craniosacral system comprises the membranes and cerebro-spinal fluid that surround and protect the brain and spinal cord. Like the Bowen Technique (see below), it encourages the

body to self heal. The best thing about cranial osteopathy and craniosacral therapy is that it is incredibly gentle, yet feels wonderfully relaxing. I had this through labour to ease the contractions and as soon after the birth as I could. Even if you give birth naturally, the positions you adopt are likely to put a huge strain on your lower back and pelvis, and an epidural is even worse. Try to have a treatment in the first few weeks after the birth.

Many therapists will come to your home if they specialise in post-natal treatment. It may cost a little more but it's worth it not to have to drive anywhere. I believe this therapy should be offered free to all babies, particularly after a difficult birth. Often the tiny little bones in a baby's skull can be out of alignment, having been compressed during birth, especially if a ventouse or forceps have been used. Even after a natural birth, after descending the birth canal, the baby may have an odd-shaped head and could be feeling pressure. Unfortunately babies can't tell you if they have a raging headache, blocked sinuses or respiratory problems, but many a fretful baby has stopped crying and begun sleeping after a couple of sessions of cranial osteopathy. To find out more and find an accredited practitioner who is experienced at working with babies and children go to **www.cranial.org.uk**. For craniosacral therapy go to the College of Cranio-Sacral Therapy (0207 586 0120, **www.ccst.co.uk**).

# The Bowen technique

The other treatment that I would say is an absolute 'must' after the rigours of childbirth is Bowen. I know I may sound like a stuck record, but throughout your child-carrying years, when you're twisting around breastfeeding, scooping up your baby or dangling your toddler on your hip, there is no finer treatment than Bowen to help realign your pelvis, neck and shoulders or your back and legs. Bowen is incredibly gentle and non-invasive and you can have a treatment as soon after birth as you want. It's also fantastic to help relieve wind and colic (see pages 139–40).

Bowen is another treatment that allegedly triggers the body to heal itself. It was devised by Australian therapist, Tom Bowen, and proved to be very successful in treating horses. It involves a barely perceptible muscle manipulation that is done over your clothes. The practitioner uses a tiny rolling movement across certain pressure points on the body and then leaves the room to allow your own body to take over the healing process.

The first time I had a Bowen treatment was when I had severe lower back pain in pregnancy. I thought I was being ripped off when I was left alone! I needn't have worried, however, as I was totally cured in one session and I now try to persuade anyone I meet who has any kind of muscular pain to try Bowen. As long as you find a good practitioner, it can work in just one or two sessions. It is excellent for pelvic pain, frozen shoulder or tennis elbow, and has even been claimed to help with hay fever and tinnitus. My tried and trusted amazing therapist is Fiona Meeks (0208 876 3010), based in south-west London. Sadly, there's only one Fiona but to find a practitioner near to you, go to **www.thebowentechnique.com**.

# Sex

I honestly can't remember having sex during the year after my first child was born and yet, unless it really was an immaculate conception, I must have done because I found out I was pregnant with the second when my first was just seven months old. Yes, I was exclusively breast-feeding, so don't believe the old chestnut about not being able to conceive while breastfeeding!

I know it's a favourite thing for women to cry out in the transition phase of labour 'You'll never touch me again!' but, once you've forgotten about the pains, your passion will eventually return. Of course, the big problem will be that, although your libido may have returned, your energy levels may not have. Often the spirit is willing but the flesh is weak and you are just too exhausted to start donning your suspenders and swinging from the rafters.

Studies show that it's quite normal to lose interest in sex for a while after childbirth, in some cases for up to a year. In any case, it would hurt like hell initially and most women choose to wait at least until their six-week post-natal check up.

A third of new mums report urinary continence problems and you'll have been advised about the benefits of pelvic floor exercises throughout pregnancy and beyond. If you fancy a gadget, you could treat yourself to a pelvic toner, a progressive resistance vaginal exerciser (**www.pelvictoner.co.uk**). The manu-facturers claim it strengthens the muscles that support the vagina, urethra, bladder, uterus and rectum. They claim it also greatly improves your sexual enjoyment and responsiveness and it's safe to use two to three months after the birth.

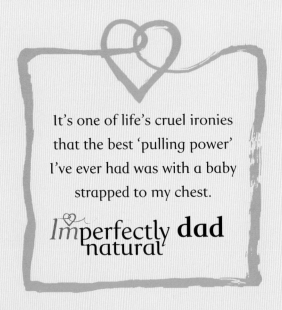

It's one of life's cruel ironies that the best 'pulling power' I've ever had was with a baby strapped to my chest.

*Im*perfectly **dad** natural

It's normal to feel cautious and concerned about resuming your sex life, particularly if your partner seems ready way before you do. You've been on quite an emotional rollercoaster ride and this can affect your feelings about sex. Try to start gently with intimate cuddles and kisses.

When you do start to think about intimacy again, you will no doubt wonder, and people will ask you constantly – how on earth do you manage it with a baby in the bed, and possibly attached to your breast for half the night? Even if your baby is sleeping soundly in his cot, you may be afraid he'll wake and cry at the crucial moment.

Interestingly, women who breastfeed and/or co-sleep with their babies report having no less sex than women who are getting up three or four times in the night, which can be even more exhausting and damaging to the libido. At least you can just roll over and give your baby a feed if he wakes. More often than not, a baby who has been used to sleeping with his parents will sleep through absolutely anything, just as he did in the womb. Many women who are breastfeeding find that when they reach orgasm, their breasts spurt out milk like a fountain! Don't be embarrassed – just aim for the ceiling!

If your baby being nearby is putting you or your partner off, don't let it! In other cultures, it's quite normal to make love with your baby awake alongside you and, no, it doesn't harm them or send them down deviant paths as adults. On the contrary, it is entirely natural and any embarrassment about it just shows how prudish and unliberated we can be in the West. (See pages 72–82 for more on sleep.)

# Returning to work

'I wanted to change the world but I couldn't find a babysitter.'

ANON

I found a fantastic 1960s black and white video in the charity shop when Sonny and Buddy were small – 'Watch with Mother'. We all love it to bits. The title alone is important as it assumes children watch the television with their mother. We laughed out loud at the Woodentops, who represented a family of a bygone age. They were the model of perfection but, it's not reality any more and we wouldn't necessarily want it to be.

We should all be given the choice of setting up family units as we wish and working as we need or wish but I do wonder if perhaps the pendulum has swung too far in the wrong direction. There seems to be the expectation that everyone must be in the workplace, women must go back to work within six weeks of childbirth and babies and children should be forced into expensive childcare facilities.

Being a very ambitious working mother, I have a lifestyle about as far removed from that of the Woodentops as you can get, so don't get me wrong. If you are a working mum who enjoys her job and has a wonderful nurturing relationship with your baby who is extremely happy to be in whatever childcare situation you have provided, then it's clear I'm not talking to you on this one. I do believe it can be possible to 'have your cake and eat it'. Women who want to work should be supported and encouraged to find flexible working hours and effective childcare that works for them. In the same breath, I would hold my hand up and praise the mother who is prepared to be a 'stay at home' mum because it's the hardest (though very fulfilling) job of all. Most importantly, women should not be pressurised and should have the choice of finding their own balance between work life and being there for their family.

If you're still on maternity leave, that day will seem a wonderfully long time away. It all comes around so quickly though and, while you have the right to change your mind, most employers want you to have made u commitment as to whether and when you're returning to work. Read the section on getting what you want from life (pages 178–86) to see how differently you may feel once your baby is born and bear that in mind when you discuss all the possibilities.

Let's take the standard approach first.

Many women, if they're enjoying their job, take the statutory time off work and plan to return. What often happens though, is that, as that day draws near, they become terrified at the thought of putting their child into day care or hiring the right nanny (more on that later). Or possibly, they simply feel like a different person to the one who left workwearing the smart maternity suit over the huge bump, carrying her baby shower gifts and cards.

It's easy to make plans on paper: Grandma will have the baby for two days, husband's sister for the other two and part-time childminder for day five. Breastfeeding, if still ongoing, can continue for a while with expressed milk and we can hire a cleaner to help with extra washing and chores. Sorted.

Sadly the reality isn't quite so simple. It's easy to plan as if the baby were a rather compliant doll rather than a very wilful little human being. Add to that the very unpredictable factor of how you will feel being a mum. If you're exhausted, as many women are for the first few months, you may barely come up for air, let alone be able to start looking for appropriate childcare. Your relative, though willing to help out occasionally, may not be so keen to take on sole charge of your baby for long stretches and you may find expressing milk is not so simple after all. Then there's the physical effort of just getting dressed (I mean in anything other than a milk-stained T-shirt and jeans, or tracky

bottoms if you can't fit into your jeans). You mustn't underestimate the effect of lack of sleep.

I'm not trying to put you off; I just want you to be realistic. I know that I'm very lucky. I chose to go back to doing radio shows only a month after having my first, doing just a few shows a week in the middle of the night (I was up anyway!). Sometimes husband and baby just tagged along. I have hilarious memories of breastfeeding between playing records and talking on air, signalling to Dad to come and take baby out of the studio in case his slurping sounds went out over the airwaves! I certainly wasn't prepared to compromise when it came to breastfeeding, so I didn't go back to my daytime radio stuff, involving longer hours, until each baby was about four months old. Still too early, I hear you say, but it was part-time. There is no way that I could have contemplated doing a full-time job five days a week until any of mine were over a year old. Women do it though and they do it admirably.

If, by the way, you're wondering how I can be into attachment parenting while discussing mothers going out to work, I don't believe the two things are incompatible at all. I have never felt any guilt whatsoever about going to work. It's what I enjoy and I am fulfilled in my work and that's a great role model to create for my kids.

Governments often seem to be forcing women back into work as early as possible after having a baby, offering incentives such as contributions towards the costs of childcare. Possibly it's just to 'cook the books' on the employment figures. Perhaps a better option might be to reward women in other ways for the incredible job they are doing. What sense does it make for a mother who is not ready, to go back to a job that is paying her only slightly more than she needs for her childcare. Wouldn't it be better to encourage mothers, or fathers if they so choose, to raise their kids themselves. They are the future generation after all and should be nurtured, where possible, in the first few formative years. Parents should be recognised for what is an astoundingly important job and not pressurised into outsourcing their childcare if they don't want to. Don't think there's a right or wrong on this issue, just get the balance right and you will make the right choices. Mum knows best!

Surveys show that each year, on average, eight and a quarter million mothers do feel it is worth facing their very real doubts and guilt to go back to work. Most of them return within eight months. Mother@work is an e-zine (**www.motheratwork.co.uk**) where you can read more about being a working mother and meet others who may have already experienced some of the issues you are facing. Denise Tyler, one of the writers, is a working mum herself. She says 'We hold an annual awards event to recognise employers who are doing that little bit extra to help working mothers get the balance right because, when you do go back, even if your workload stays the same, your hours won't. Your working day will be dictated by childcare so, if you need to, ask for flexible working hours. There are many ways to work flexibly and you have a right to apply by law now – check out the DTI's site (**www.dti.gov.uk**) on flexible working for how to go about it.

## A different hat

What if you can't face it or the sums simply don't add up once you've paid for the childcare? Well, then you'll need to start being creative and decide how you can stay at home, look after your children and earn money at the same time. Don't make the mistake of thinking that while you're tapping away on the computer or sticking stamps on a million mailouts, your little cherub will simply lie and gurgle. He'll demand lots of attention and involvement. We went through a phase when Sonny was seven months old when my husband thought it would be simple to have him in his carry cot while he did some work in his studio. Well, the lying in the carry cot lasted about an hour, and then became a crawling baby picking up CDs and trying to eat them while DH tried in vain to concentrate on recording music!

People are also, slowly but surely (and I hope this book will help), moving away from huge conglomerates for every last item we purchase and looking for more locally sourced, hand-crafted, fairly traded and more unique produce. This trend has led to a huge growth in small businesses, some of them literally one mum in her kitchen making stuff while the toddler plays (or helps!). Enter then the world of the working at home mums or WAHM, as they like to be called. Many start by simply making kit for their own children – toys, slings etc. Others embark on all manner of entrepreneurial extravaganzas. Some I know have found that they have a talent for holistic services such as Reiki, Bowen or even astrology. From humble beginnings can spring a profitable business.

What struck me when I looked into this world was the huge generosity and sharing that seemed to be going on; both a sharing of information with other mums starting out in business and a sharing of resources. There are several websites dedicated to WAHM, including marketplaces where you can promote and sell your work. One of the lifelines for working at home mums is being able to advertise their wares for free on sites such as Netmums (**www.net mums.co.uk**), UK Parents (**www.uk parents.co.uk**) or **www.mumszone. co.uk**. For budding entrepreneurs, there's an excellent opportunity to run your own 'online shop' through **www.mumzmall. co.uk**. Net services such as eBay and PayPal are invaluable. To get organised, there are some fantastic wall planners and diaries from **www.organisedmum.co.uk**.

Since becoming aware of it, I now look at one of WAHM marketplaces on the net before I go to any high street shop because I'd rather support a working at home mum. The chances are, her product will be cheaper and far more funky.

Netmums did a survey recently called The Great Work Debate, which showed that eighty-eight per cent of those working full-time would rather work part-time or stay at home with their children. By contrast, sixty-eight per cent of those who were self employed felt this was the ideal solution for combining work and home life. Of the 4,000 mums surveyed, the happiest group were those working part-time or running their own businesses.

Here's Phillipa's experience. She set up a net business selling baby slings. 'I began looking into setting up a business from home. I was lucky to have great advice and support from other small business owners who I found through various online parenting forums. I was at home anyway and had the time to treat it as a hobby initially. Now, a couple of years down the line, it's much more successful than I'd ever have imagined and keeps me very busy.'

'There are lots of wonderful things about being a WAHM. I can always be there for the children when they need me; I can work in my pyjamas, manage my own time and don't have to answer to anyone. However, there are downsides too. Taking a holiday is very difficult as I don't have any employees so it's hard to leave the business. Also, working from home, it can be hard to switch off and relax, and my husband complains about the amount of time I spend on the laptop. Running a home-based business isn't the easy job that some people think it is. It takes an awful lot of time and effort to build it up into something profitable but I'm very proud of what I've achieved. When I get feedback from happy customers with happy babies who are enjoying their slings, it makes all the hard work worthwhile.' Visit **www. littlepossums.co.uk**, the UK Baby Sling Specialists.

## Downshifting

Sometimes, women decide to take it one step further and actually reduce the amount they need to live on in order to eliminate the necessity for two incomes. I used to think that downshifting meant moving to a smaller property, perhaps because the children had left home or you'd divorced and suddenly found that a one-bedroom apartment was sufficient. In fact, it's much more than changing your life just for financial reasons, it's about making a conscious lifestyle choice which can often result in a happier, more relaxed, greener and, yes, more financially viable way of life.

Writer and broadcaster Tracey Smith explains: 'Downshifting equals slowing down to a lower gear. In everyday terms,

# I'm perfectly natural parent

**Your name, age group, age of children** Nicola Haxell, aged 29. Children are 12, 10, 2 and 6 months.

**Occupation?** I run **www.ninny noodlenoo.com** selling wooden toys, Barefoot Books and organic children's clothing and toiletries and co-run **www.donny nutters.co.uk**, selling a selection of organic/natural family and household goods.

**Birth experiences – natural/assisted?** All my children were born in hospital and were 'natural' births (as natural as being in a hospital can be). I did have gas and air on number 4, which made me feel very woozy.

**Did the baby's birth impact in any way on the first few weeks – positively or negatively?** It's the broken nights that are hardest, I do like my sleep. He (WHO?) slept mostly in bed with me still hanging on to the food source!

**Your emotional state for the first six months?** Tired, but more to do with supporting my eldest son (who is diagnosed with Aspergers Syndrome) than dealing with a new baby, who's easy in comparison.

**When did your figure return – did you exercise?** Return? It took years to get back down to a size 12 after my second son, I went up to a size 20 after my daughter and was around a size 18 when I became pregnant again, and I'm still hovering around that now. I don't expect to be super-slim, that isn't something I find important in life, but I do need to shed some pounds. I exercise by walking everywhere but clearly I'm not doing enough (eating less would likely help).

**Breastfeeding experience?** I started to breastfeed my eldest but got no support whatsoever so switched to bottlefeeding after a few months. The key to successful breastfeeding is to have a good support network. I was 26 when I had my daughter and had friends who had breastfed successfully. In addition I was able to access support from the La Leche League. I breastfed my daughter for 17 months.

**Nappies – if cloth, which type do your prefer and why?** Definitely cloth for me and mine! I've had a selection over the years and really like Tots Bots. I also have a large amount of Terry squares which come in very useful, use Motherease wraps and have a selection of fleece liners.

**First foods – homemade purees or jars?** Homemade – even when I was only 17, I made food for my children. I do buy jars occasionally. I re-use them for storing homemade food in (which means I've glass rather than plastic containers).

**What's in your medicine cupboard for the children?** I don't really do 'conventional' medicine. I use a Helios First Aid kit, I have Rescue Remedy (which I carry around in my bag) and usually arnica. Sniffles are usually given honey and lemon and bunged up noses are steamed with eucalyptus and hot water.

**What is your own diet like? Favourite superfoods?** I eat A LOT of fruit, I love raspberries and blueberries. I now have an allotment where I have planted 16 raspberry canes to feed my raspberry habit!

**What do you do to keep 'sane'? What do you do for 'me' time?** I don't really have any 'me' time but I knit, something that for me has a meditative quality.

**What is your favourite holistic treatment/ therapy?** I've never been in a position to treat myself to one, not even a massage. One day I will but it'll have to wait until Ned has stopped breastfeeding and I can find someone who'll stay still long enough to watch all the children whilst I do it.

**How do you deal with challenging behaviour?**
By distraction and discussion. I will also ask my elder ones to go to their room when we're both particularly worked up to give us both the opportunity to calm down.

**As a family how green are you? 10 is dark and leafy, 1 is a faint hint of peppermint.** Probably around 5 – we'd do more, but my husband isn't as enthusiastic as I am.

**Do you recycle everything?** The council picks up paper, cans, glass, clothing (although I take ours to the local charity shop, or chop it up to make something else with) and printer cartridges. We compost what we can.

**What are your favourite simple activities to do with babies?** Babywearing. It's great. I have a wrap sling (a Storchenwiege) that I got from **www.baby armadillo.com** and it's the best baby buy I've made. He loves being carried around and it means he can take part in a small way in everything I do, which keeps him very happy. I sing: when I'm doing the washing up, when I'm cleaning, when I'm pottering about. Ned loves that.

**How much TV do you allow your child to watch?**
Very little, although I have rescinded a little recently. I really dislike adverts and will actively stop my children watching child-targeted adverts. My eldest son has difficulty separating fact from fiction and needs support when watching films.

**How do you feel about commercial toys/branding – are you first in the queue at midnight on Christmas Eve for this year's must-have toy?**
Absolutely not. I set up Ninny Noodle Noo because I wanted something different. The conditions in which some top-selling toys are made are far from ideal, the amount of plastic used is an environmental nightmare and the aggressive marketing just plain wrong in my opinion. I like simple toys, wooden and cloth – things that can be mended or recycled. I looked for toys that come from sustainable hardwood forests, non-toxic dyes (food grade) and come in minimal packaging. I've also made some toys. I think it's also important to remember that our children abound with imagination and sometimes the most simple of objects can provide the most magical of experiences. The trusty cardboard box can be a castle, a boat, a car, a house, a cave – so many things. Add some pieces of material and you have a sail for your boat, a skirt, a cape, with the help of some sticks (or a clothes horse) a tent or house – provide some basic props for hours of fun.

**Your top three tips for imperfectly natural parenting?** Patience – you can never have too much patience. Confidence – in yourself and your choices for your family. Optimism – look forward with hope, don't dwell on mistakes and regret, learn and move forward.

**What are your imperfections?** I spend rather more time on the PC than I feel I should (especially as I'm on a rather high horse with regards to the children using it). I sometimes bite a bit too quickly when my eldest is trying to argue and yes, I sneak bits of their chocolate when they're not looking…

**Do you keep 'all the balls' in the air? If not, why? Is it lack of time?** I try and generally succeed. The major challenge for me is learning to live with my eldest son who can be a prickly person and having the courage to admit that I need some outside advice and support – because I'm a doer, not a taker.

**Anything else you'd like to share to help towards an imperfectly natural world?** Give green a go!

that means trimming your time and finance budgets to a more comfortable level. Dip your toes in gently; make simple changes, analyse how good you feel after them, then "lean towards the green" with things like recycling, reusing, composting and so on, which is great news. In short, you Slow Down and Green Up!' For suggestions, see www.Downshifting Week.com.

# Childcare options

My view is that in an ideal world, children should be looked after in their own home. I've never fancied carting my baby off to day nurseries where I can never be quite sure that she is getting one-on-one attention when she needs it. I certainly don't buy into the sociability argument of nurseries. Babies and toddlers need familiar faces and surroundings, not a sea of equipment and lots of other little people they don't know. I do appreciate, though, that it's way too simplistic to write off all day care. It may seem idealistic, but all I wanted was for my eighteen-month-old son to be at home, choosing whether he wanted to help cook beans or pasta, and being allowed to stand on his FunPod (see page 124) to do the washing up.

Before you scream at me, I have close friends whose situations have been very different. One of them has two sons she sent to a day nursery at about three months while she went back to work full-time. Her boys seemingly loved it and have been very happy. So, while I wouldn't have done it her way, she couldn't have walked in my shoes either but I believe that, with any kind of childcare situation, there is always going to be an element of compromise between the baby's needs and your own.

I buy into the theory that babies should really just be 'tagging along' (see page 195). If only that weren't cloud cuckoo land! If only we did all live in lovely communities or extended family situations only a short walk or bike ride to work, or we could be self-sufficient within our homes. I certainly did not have the luxury of an extended family; in fact, I didn't have anyone who lived anywhere near me. So, having decided against a day nursery and, having no relatives to help with childcare, I had to consider the other options.

## Nannies

Good nannies are worth every penny they are paid but it's a big expense and you have to deal with their tax and national insurance, which is scary, though help is at hand at on www.nanny tax.co.uk.

## Childminders

I looked at registered childminders who look after children in their own homes. I visited a few and I liked the fact that they were usually just mums getting on with life, often with babies and toddlers in tow. Flexibility was often a problem though because of their own family commitments.

## Mother's help

A mother's help isn't usually trained or qualified as a nanny but that didn't worry me. I set out to find another mother who had no formal qualifications or experience whatsoever but who'd brought up kids and had mothering skills. A mother's help fitted in very well with my attachment parenting philosophy too as I felt I needed someone who was willing to come into my home and do pretty much what I would have done if I'd been there, such as housework (steady on, not too much), shopping, cooking and playing with the baby or toddler. We found a wonderful local woman who worked for us on a self-employed, part-time basis for six years and we're still friends.

## Au pairs

Once we had four children, we realised we needed an au pair (the legal definition is 'another pair of hands') and, while this was a steep learning curve because I was concerned about having someone live in, it proved to be the best thing we ever did. Our au pair keeps the house in a reasonable state and absolutely loves the children. She has become fluent in our language and our children have learnt a few words

of hers. I used a great website **www.au pairworld.net**.

As a rule of thumb, treat au pairs well and they will treat you well. Set out their obligations and don't be tempted to overwork them. There has to be an element of mutual respect and they do live as part of the family. As long as you can offer an au pair her own room and board, this is the least expensive option.

# Support

If you are not lucky enough to have extended family living nearby, childcare for just short periods of time can be an issue. Again you have options.

## Trading your time

When I had my second son, the best present we received, apart from all the soft bunnies and silver first tooth boxes, was a card from a friend containing a voucher for one whole night's babysitting – even staying the night, if required! Boy, what a gift!

Time spent looking after children is a valuable commodiy, and one that it makes sense to trade, so make friends with local mums. It doesn't matter too much if all you have in common is your kids, as long as they are entirely trustworthy. You can trade tea-times. When my third baby was born and DH was away for a couple of days, I remember ringing a friend and offering to look after her children for an afternoon, evening or whatever she needed, in return for her coming over – I simply wanted to soak in the bath! We laugh about it now but you'll be in a similar situation one day, believe me!

## Babysitting circles

These can work brilliantly. If there isn't one in your area, why don't you try setting one up? If you join your local branch of the NCT (**www.national childbirthtrust. co.uk**), you will almost certainly find that there is a circle or enough local people who would love to start one up. No money needs to change hands as it's all done on a points system. It requires one volunteer to be the co-ordinator, who keeps track of the points and then, in theory, every time you ask for a sitter you'll need to return the favour. The beauty of this system is that, apart from being an entirely reciprocal arrangement, it helps to build that community spirit, you know the person who is looking after your children and because he or she is also a parent, they should know how to look after a child and what to do in a crisis.

While we're on the subject of babysitting, by the way, do make time to go out with your partner, even if it's only to have a drink for an hour. Put on your glad rags every week or so and you'll start to feel human again.

# Getting what you want from life

'Children carry less baggage than we do so run faster, follow them.'

KAREN REVANS

So you're a new mum or perhaps a second- or third- time mum, you have your 'bundle of joy' and everything is perfect – right? Probably not. I'm not talking about the very serious illness that is post-natal depression (see pages 19–20) but how you are feeling about you. Everyone will be asking about the baby and you'll get a reasonable amount of attention for the first few weeks too, but what about after that? What about when life settles down into some kind of routine or normality, albeit an entirely different one to life 'BC' (before children)? I'm sure you will have seen newspaper surveys and 'how to' books, heard of workshops and websites and even watched mainstream TV series about happiness. We're all asking the question: 'What makes us happy?' It won't surprise you to know that there's no one definitive answer and we all have different aspirations, but there are a number of contributing factors. The interesting thing is that these aspirations and dreams, some of which we may have had since childhood, can change completely with the birth of our own children. The surveys and TV series have found that love doesn't necessarily make us happy, nor does being in our dream job. They did find, however, that the happiest people seemed to be those with fulfilled family or community relationships. The greatest cause of unhappiness came down to being lonely and having very little human contact.

Psychologist and author John F. Schumaker wrote an excellent book called **In Search of Happiness: Understanding an Endangered State of Mind** (Penguin). In an excellent article entitled 'The Happiness Conspiracy' for New Internationalist magazine (July 2006), he says: 'Sustainable happiness harks back to Greek philosophies in viewing ethical living as a legitimate vehicle for happiness. Compassion, in particular, plays a central role. In part it rests on the truth that we can be happy in planting the seeds of happiness, even if we might miss the harvest.' Isn't that interesting? What we're doing when we bring our wonderful babies into the world is giving them the gift of life. That's why I don't buy into the 'older mother is bad' theory. The reality is that often, once you've had a baby, you may feel quite isolated. You'll be extremely busy and, of course, you can enjoy your little one, but you're important too and there will be times when you may think 'What about me? Where do I fit into all of this?' Initially, babies are all-consuming and all your energies will go into nurturing them. You'll just be grateful if someone offers to hold the baby while you have a shower or make a phone call but, as the months tick by, you may start to think, once the baby is at nursery, school or college, 'What do I want for myself?' So, if you do find yourself wanting a change of direction, do you just hope for the best and accept that what will be will be? Of course not! Think positively and take control.

Cosmic Ordering became fashionable when Noel Edmonds claimed it had helped him reclaim his successful TV career. It's something I've spoken about a lot because, although I hadn't heard it called that before, I think cosmic ordering is actually what I do, though I choose to call it visual-isation. Other phrases are positive thinking or manifestation. It's ridiculous that it all sounds so 'out there', as it's simply about putting your mental efforts (as well as your actual efforts) into getting what you want. And that's where the problem often lies, as many people don't actually know what it is they want. It's easy to drift through life in a boring job or the wrong relationship, making poor choices and constantly complaining about your 'lot'. Somehow, you can't seem to progress because you can't identify what it is you really want or, in some cases, need. It's quite common for women to have their first child and then seriously to reassess where their lives are going.

After the initial babymoon period has passed, it is quite usual to feel really unfocused and unsure of your future from a personal perspective. Some women just don't feel as though they are the same person they were before they had a child

and this can seem a bit frightening. Your whole world has changed, your body has changed and you are responsible for another human being 24/7. Your relationship with your partner has a new dynamic then, blow me, you start wondering if you want to go back to work or ever look at a computer, switchboard, classroom or whatever work is for you, again.

This may be a time to evaluate and there are whole libraries on the subject of achieving your dreams and manifesting what you want. Brandon Bays is a leading author in the field, as is Susan Jeffers, whose book **Feel the Fear and Do It Anyway** was a life-changing book for me. She talks about positive affirmations and the need to repeat them daily. Her theory is that we should view it as a mind workout in the same way that many people exercise in a gym. We need to think positively, work out what we want and affirm it regularly. If you hate the word affirmation, you're not alone, so just call it wishing, if you prefer.

How do you work out what it is you want? A great first step is to draw a diagram at your 'wheel of life' on the Wellbeing network (**www.wellbeingnetwork.com**). Use this fantastic diagnostic tool to see what stage you're at. Obviously, the wheel has several spokes for all the important areas including health, relationships family, friends, work or career, leisure and relaxation, contribution (how much you give to society, whether financially or in

time) and so on. Think of the number ten as being total satisfaction and number one as very unfulfilled, and then assign a score to each of the spokes. In an ideal world, we'd have a reasonably high number in each of the categories, but many of us may realise, for example, that we are very happy at work and score a nine or a ten but, when it comes to family or leisure time, we may score a miserable two. Being aware of how you need to redress the balance is the first step.

The next step is to visualise what you want to happen. Set out your goals or place an 'order'. That is it! I did it years ago when I was a jobbing session singer with very little work. I wrote down a list of about seven or eight dreams (our brains can't cope with many more, so don't be greedy) and the wish list included aspects of personal stuff like family goals and my career. It all came to fruition, though not necessarily in the way I asked for it.

If you know exactly what you want, it's very important to be specific. There is an old saying that reminds us to be careful what we wish for because it may just come true. Make sure that you have thought through what it is you really want. Susan Jeffers talks of the guy who spent his life climbing the ladder to success only to find when he reached the top that the ladder had been pitched against the wrong wall. Don't say vaguely 'I want to be a millionaire', as that's unlikely to happen. Remember, it needs to be for the highest good of all concerned, so there's no point asking for a million pounds from a successful bank robbery! State how you want to make your money. Anyway, you wouldn't want your wealthy best friend to die, leaving you their fortune in order to fulfil that wish.

It's okay to dream a little and be creative, so your wish list might say, for example: 'I am a full-time mum and I am financially okay; I am the creative director of a successful advertising firm; I am living in my dream home in the countryside.' It's even better if you can give more detail like 'I am living in my dream home in St Ives in Cornwall. It has roses around the door and a small, south-facing patio. My children are happy in their local school.'

I know it sounds a bit barking but, honestly, it works! If you can't do the rather American repeating of affirmations, write down the goals and look at them regularly. A good time is just before you go to bed as, while you sleep, your subconscious will go to work on your instructions and start to create ways to bring all your dreams to reality.

When you read your list, don't be judgemental. Try to ignore the 'this could never happen to me' thought that will pop into your head. Often, our inner voice is what sabotages us. We've each got a good fairy on one shoulder and a bad on the other and, if you want to control your self-sabotage, read Susan Jeffers's books – all of them.

## Feng shui

A few years ago, we needed to rent out our house. On the advice of our favourite feng shui practitioner, Dinka Cinnamon (**www.fengshui4you.co.uk**), we wrote down a fictional name on an envelope, addressed to our home as if that family were already living there and included a fake posting date (approximately one week after we needed to move out). We put it in our 'wealth corner' next to a picture of our house, the 'to let' blurb from the estate agent and a candle which we lit daily to affirm our intentions. The next day a family came to view the property and told us that they needed to move in on the exact date we had specified. Don't get too spooked though, their name wasn't the one we'd made up!

So, is it that easy? Well, yes, but your wishes must remain rooted in reality as it's unlikely you'll become an airline pilot if you're terrified of flying. Also, it's probably not for everyone's highest good if you put all your intentions into marrying Tom Cruise, especially if he's already taken. But, within reason and with a little reality, anything is possible. Of course, you need to put a bit of physical effort in too. If your dream is to become a bestselling author, get writing; if you are looking for a partner, be absolutely specific.

I have a widowed friend who wrote down exactly the man she wanted to meet: his height, build, looks, wealth, personality – everything. A few days later, a friend in London invited her to dinner to meet her colleague, Jack. That same day, she had an email from a girlfriend in America that said: 'I've just met a colleague of my husband's who was over here on business. He's from London and he's perfect for you – his name is Jack.' At first she didn't imagine it could possibly be the same man, but it turned out it was. The 'universe' was making sure, doubly sure, that she got her dream. They married six months later and he is everything she wrote on her list. The only thing she forgot to specify was his hair colour. It turned out he was bald but that didn't worry her at all!

Stick your wish list somewhere you can look at it often and, if your goals change, just add to it or create another. You can produce different lists for different aspects of your life. My friend, Cordelia, made an action sports treasure map with lots of snowboarding pictures and, a few weeks later, was invited on a free press trip to Courchevel to report on a free-ride competition. The hire snowboard was exactly the same as the one she'd put on the wish list! She stayed in five-star hotels and was wined and dined by PR people – total magic!

You can also complete a community wish list or even a global one, manifesting everything from clean water to helping Africa and world peace! Do it with the kids, however young, and inspire them to think about what they want and to affirm positive images and dreams. It's fantastic to introduce children to this concept early on so that, when they're finding their way as teenagers and adults, they'll already be used to harnessing the power of their mind.

I have tried to encourage my children to use their subconscious mind from a very young age to help them when they felt ill. I remember lying with my second child, Buddy, when he was about three and a half and had tummy ache. We did a little guided visualisation. I asked him to see where a little bug – we called him Mr Pain – was wandering around his tummy and making it hurt, but then a waterfall came and washed Mr Pain away. At this point, I'd make gentle whooshing movements on his tummy. Then I told him that all that was left was a lovely glowing white light all around him that made his tummy feel so much better.Don't worry if, like me, you're no J K Rowling – any story will do, as long as it gives the child back his power and calms his fear. Usually, the pain went away or, at least, he was no longer so anxious and stressed.

It's well documented that positive thinking and visualisation have a huge impact on patients receiving radiotherapy treatment. When a girlfriend of mine needed treatment for breast cancer, she devised her own mental picture of her favourite flower being buffeted by the wind. While this battle raged and the petals seemed to be about to come off, she visualised the sun coming out, the wind calming and the flower remaining intact and beautiful. Her treatment was completely successful and she has now been in great health for over eight years.

## Being 'in your power'

Felicity Evans is an amazingly inspirational woman and special needs teacher (**www.naturekids.co.uk**) and she is the person who first introduced me to the concept of being 'in your own power'. She is reminded of it daily because her job and, she believes the job of all successful parents, is to help children to be 'in their power'. A few years ago, she knew that I had been called in for a meeting at work and had a strong intuition that I may be about to be fired or, in any case, some aspect of my work would change, not necessarily in my favour. I was feeling nervous and financially threatened and would have gone into that meeting with the air of an underdog. Thank God for Felicity.

First, she reminded me that, whatever the outcome, I'd created this situation myself for a reason. Even if I didn't know what that reason was yet, I should go to that interview 'in my power', looking and feeling both confident and optimistic. I realised that she was right and took a totally different approach. I went in feeling totally confident. Then – here's the best bit (remember this if anyone tries to intimidate you) – she said 'Just imagine them in nappies and picture them in a, shall we say, slightly compromising position!'

Well, the meeting was indeed to inform me that I was no longer needed though, of course, it wasn't as simple as that. Nothing ever is. I sat down and looked my boss in the eye, and it was clear that she was uncomfortable and I was flying. I formed a hilarious mental picture of her wearing a huge, fluffy real nappy with a big cartoon-style safety pin. I asked whether she was aware of the benefits I could bring to the company, and then went on to outline my proposal. The end result was that I went away with a better offer, something that, without even realising it, I had needed to create for myself. As I went out of the door, I took one last look at that top businesswoman in her big nappy and delivered my parting shot ....'By the way, a pay rise would be nice.' I got one. I really believe that had I gone in the day before Felicity's chat, the outcome would have been very different. Certainly the balance of power would have been reversed.

This is a fantastic technique to use on anyone who tries to bully you, and bullies are not just children, there are many in the workplace and, some would say, in politics too. I've even known new mothers reduced to tears by health visitors' admonitions!

Felicity recommends to children that they also diffuse conflict situations by imagining their aggressor in a pink tutu or a big nappy. Take away the victim and there's no one to persecute. It's a wonderful thing for you and your children to find ways of being strong in yourselves and to help you all feel positive, powerful and balanced.

Now you're a parent, you're responsible for another human being and it's an awesome responsibility. I know that you want your child to be healthy and happy and to have good self-esteem, and building strong self-esteem in your children begins with your

An inspirational book to have on your shelf is **Meditations and Positive Thoughts for Pregnancy and Birth** (Piatkus Books), a collection of affirmations by Gilli Moorhawk. It's also worth reading **Cosmic Ordering** by Barbel Mohr. Another book to help with getting what you want is Anthony Robbins's **Unleashing the Power Within.**

own sense of worth. It may well be that becoming a mother has changed you forever but I wouldn't mind betting it has changed you for the better. I think that, along with most of my childless friends and colleagues, I was fairly selfish before I had my first child, but I don't know of many mothers who are selfish when it comes to their children. Indeed, they would probably sacrifice everything for their child's well being. Don't sacrifice your own wellbeing though. You will be a much more effective role model if you are well adjusted and happy. When they're grown up, what kind of memories do you want your kids to have of their mum? That she always kept the house spotlessly clean? That she sacrificed her own career and was miserable staying at home but made great meals? Or that she was very real and didn't get everything right (imperfect may be the operative word) but she sure as heck had a great laugh!

## OUTGROWN

It is both sad and a relief to fold so carefully
her outgrown clothes and line up the little
   worn shoes
of childhood, so prudent, scuffed and
   particular.
It is both happy and horrible to send them
   galloping
back tappity-tap along the misty chill path
   into the past.
It is both a freedom and a prison, to be
   outgrown
by her as she towers over me as thin as
   a sequin

in her Doc Martens and her pretty skirt,
because just as I work out how to be a
    mother
she stops being a child.
**Penelope Shuttle**

# Another baby?

'Having a family is like having a bowling
alley installed in your brain.'
                        MARTIN MULL

## Contraception

I really do believe that all forms of the
contraceptive pill are a hugely bad idea.
My theory is that messing with your
hormones on a daily basis is using a
sledgehammer to crack a nut. Most
couples simply do not, with the best will
in the world, have sex frequently enough
to warrant messing up their body's natural
rhythm. It's not an easy choice, I know,
but the pill would be last on my list of
contraception methods.

Natural family planning (NFP) involves
identifying and working around your
body's natural signs of fertility. A little
bit unreliable, you might think, but NFP
experts claim it has as good a success
rate as other methods. See **www.fpa.
org.uk/guide/contracep/natural.htm**
for more information. A good book to
read is Toni Weshler's **Taking Charge
of Your Fertility**.

## Trying to conceive

Although it may seem unlikely if you've just
had a difficult birth, there will probably
come a time when you'll discuss having
another baby. Interestingly, it doesn't
always follow that, just because you've
had one baby, you will be able to conceive
again on command. I know of a couple
who have a gorgeous daughter aged nine
and they have been trying for the last eight
years to give her a brother or sister. Sadly,
there is little sympathy for the couple who
have one child already, but having one
baby doesn't diminish the desire for
another – my friends have spent a fortune
on IVF and tried every trick in the book.
The irony is that, while the nation is
allegedly under threat of overpopulation by
pregnant teenagers, when you try to get
pregnant, mother nature may have other
ideas altogether.

As with so many problems and ailments,
this one may come back to your diet. If
it is not nutritionally sound, the chances
are you will find it harder to conceive. It's
advisable to take folic acid even before
you try to get pregnant and you should
address your levels of important vitamins
and minerals. If possible, see a qualified
nutritionist. To find one, contact the
British Association of Nutritional
Therapists (**www.bant.org**). It is also
important to address any smoking habit
and alcohol consumption as these can
both affect fertility.

'Having one baby doesn't diminish the desire for another'

> We had been kind of 'short' with each other for a while, but I now know this was the famous 'hormone havoc' taking hold. It was almost divorce for putting a fork in the knife compartment. If there're any blokes reading this, don't let this put you off – I now know, being a father of four, that this is all PERFECTLY NORMAL.

Yoga therapy is recommended for fertility problems and I do know someone who puts her conception down to practising yoga. It's excellent for the pelvic area generally and resting in a shoulder stand immediately after sex is believed to aid conception. Sadly, I'm way too imperfect and unfit to be able to manage a shoulder stand but you can always take the lazy option. Straight after sex, you need to hang on to that fluid, so prop your derrière up on several pillows so that your legs are higher than you head or, better still, turn around on your bed, put your legs up on the wall and lie back for ten minutes or so.

It's too big a topic to deal with here, but if you know you have a mouthful of amalgam fillings, think of the potential toxicity. If you're considering amalgam removal, you will need a specialist holistic dentist and a full mineral support programme.

Foresight, the Association for the Promotion of Preconceptual Care (**www.foresight-preconception.org.uk**) offers help and information plus hair and mineral analysis that can show up reasons why you may be unable to conceive. Another very helpful website is Pink for a Girl (**www.pinkforagirl.com**), which isn't just about trying for a girl!

One of the best ways to be aware of your own fertility is to take your temperature and chart your vaginal mucus (sorry to be so graphic!). Even if you aren't trying to determine which sex the baby will be, you can use the chart to see when you're most likely to be ovulating and you can aim to have sex around that time. Charts are available from **www.fpa.org.uk**.

Having said all of that, babies come when they're meant to and nature has a clever way of making it happen, sometimes when we're least expecting it. All that's needed is for you to relax. You can buy a 'help to conceive' relaxation CD from **www.natal hypnotherapy.co.uk**. There's also the theory that fertility has connections with the phases of the moon. If that's not too cosmic for you, check out **www.goddess mums.com**.

## Pregnant again?

Congratulations! Pregnancy is not an illness – our bodies were designed to give birth but that doesn't mean it's necessarily an easy process. Over the years, as a race, we have done much to alter the shape of our bodies, reduce the amount of physical work we do and, of course, clog up our system with processed foods, often resulting in a deficiency of important nutrients in the process. This is something we need to redress if we want a natural birth. I can point you nowhere better than Dr Gowri Motha (**www.gentle birthmethod.com**) for all you need to know. She is, without doubt, the most important force on everything connected with pregnancy and natural childbirth.

Unfortunately, there is far too much for me to cover here, so you're going to have to wait for my book on pregnancy and birth, save to say that one of my main passions in life is to encourage women to prepare for pregnancy. As Gowri says in the intro to her excellent book **Gentle Birth Method** '(as) pregnant women (we) spend longer preparing the nursery for the baby than our bodies. We sigh over wallpaper

swatches, pore over name books and coo over cots without once thinking about conditioning ourselves for the birth.'

I found self-hypnosis and visualisation very helpful in pregnancy for achieving the births I wanted. Gowri offers classes in the London area and you should also check out Maggie Howell, an inspirational clinical hypnotherapist and mother of three on **www.natalhypnotherapy.co.uk**.

Being pregnant when you already have a child will be a different experience. Sadly, you won't have the luxury of putting your feet up so often. There will be times when you feel it's impossible to drag your own bloated, pregnant body up a staircase, alone carrying your heavy toddler as well. If this doesn't sound too ridiculous, what I highly recommend is that you really enjoy your body and involve your toddler. My first little boy loved to put his hand on my huge tummy and feel his little brother kicking. Make sure you get lots of support from like-minded mums during pregnancy A couple of great forums where the members are very supportive are **www.pregnancyforum.co.uk** and **www.picklesworld.com**.

If you're preparing your body for a natural birth, it will be very important to consider where to have your baby. In an ideal world, I would have had home births, as I believe that's the most natural environment in which to give birth. Because I was so ancient when I had my first, I was nervous and went the private hospital route but was determined to have natural water births and threw money at it. I often tell people I've had babies instead of holidays as I've spent what most people spend on a fortnight in the Caribbean employing reflexologists and birth gurus in a very holistic birth unit.

Home birth has been an amazing experience for many of my friends. You will feel none of the panic associated with trying to decide when to leave for the hospital and none of the pressures of an overcrowded labour ward. See **www.home birth.org.uk**. You can hire a birthing pool and set it up in your living room too (see **www.gentlewater.co.uk**).

> **TOP TIP**
> Get some gorgeous pictures of your bare bump! I would never in a million years consider taking my kit off for a photo but professionally done pregnancy photos are very tasteful and somehow magical.
> I particularly love Tina Bolton's photography
> **www.tinabolton.co.uk**

The best bit is that the midwives attending will be all yours for however long the process takes. On that note, by the way, I can't recommend highly enough that you join the initiative called One Mother One Midwife (**www.onemotheronemidwife. org.uk** – it is exactly what it says on the tin). The health service desperately needs more midwives so that each woman can have the birth of her choice. The midwife should be someone she knows and trusts, who has seen her throughout her pregnancy. And if you think that this couldn't be cost-effective, consider the savings the NHS could make in the long term, with less intervention, less costly Caesareans and less money spent on aftercare for babies and mothers, not to mention fewer cases of post-natal depression.

A poor birth experience can have a devastating effect on the health and wellbeing of mothers and babies, and it makes no sense to continue down the intervention route just to meet the schedule of the obstetrician on duty. Most midwives are wonderful, loving people with a vocation, and a high percentage of those who have left the profession have said they would return if they could have a one-on-one relationship. Look at **www.independentmidwives. org.uk** to find a midwife in your area. Some are NHS-funded, others are private. The Birthlight Trust (**www.birthlight. com**) is an educational charity that

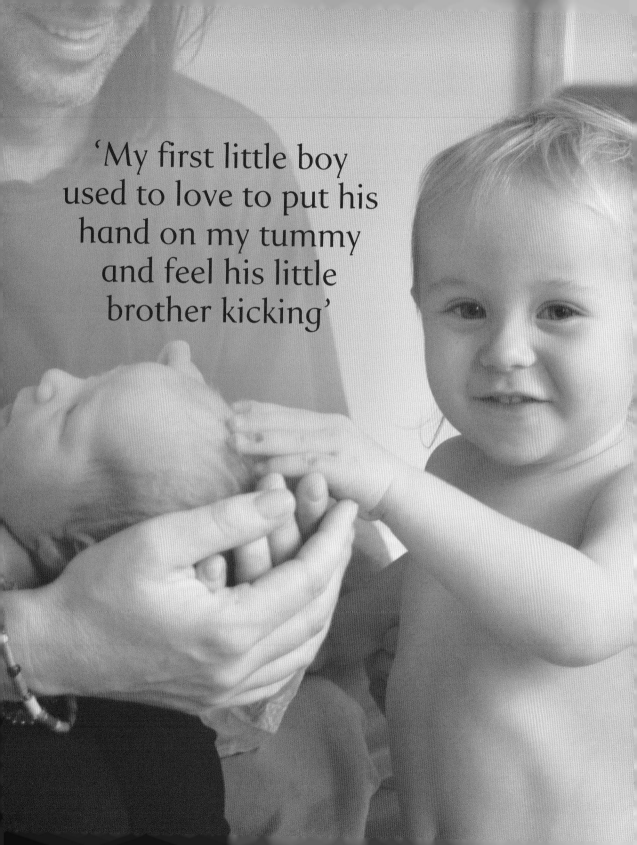

'My first little boy used to love to put his hand on my tummy and feel his little brother kicking'

promotes an integrated, holistic approach to pregnancy, birth and babyhood. Its main objective is to enhance wellbeing and enjoyment for parents and their babies before and after birth. They offer excellent antenatal yoga classes, if you can get to them, as well as some wonderful yoga classes for mothers and babies or toddlers.

## Jealousy

Whatever the age of your first child, when you have your second, they will be knocked for six. I could see the bottom fall out of Sonny's world when the new baby appeared and it's completely under-standable. They have been king of their castle for their whole life and, suddenly, another prince appears who is constantly attached to Mummy and seems to be getting all the attention and masses of presents. It's hugely important to spend time alone with your first child, even while you're trying to bond with the new baby. Make sure that visitors make a fuss of the older child, before they look at the new baby too.

As they both get older, one of the best books to help with kids constantly fighting and arguing is Siblings Without Rivalry: How to Help Your Children Live Together So You Can Live Too by Adele Faber, Elaine Mazlish and Kimberly Ann Coe.

# I*m*perfectly natural parent

**Your name, age group, age of children** Karl Hampson, 38, with a daughter, Ella, 22 months.

**Occupation?** IT Business Director.

**Your emotional state for the first six months?** Ecstatic and complete. I guess I'd never thought about how I would feel during that time until I was actually there. It made me realise how shallow my materialistic desires in life (up to that time) were. I was proud of how well Lynne, my wife, dealt with the whole thing. Having been through the pregnancy and birth in which I felt like a passenger a lot of the time, all of a sudden I could get involved. Breastfeeding obviously reduced that level of involvement to some degree but I tried very hard to bond and be as involved with Ella as possible. Working from home and seeing Ella every day made this a really special time (and it still is).

**How was your relationship with your partner?** Good, but clearly it was into a new phase. Lynne was understandably more emotional at times and having Ella now meant she had less time for me. But I was prepared for that and just accepted it. It wasn't a problem, there was too much to do!

**What do you hear yourself saying to your children often that you wish you didn't?** Questions that come out of frustration or not thinking, which I know she can't answer, like 'Why did you do that?'

**Do you consider fair-trade/ethical trading?** I do consider it, but (for example) I refuse to drink average-tasting coffee just to be green. My general philosophy is a balance between doing the right thing and not paying over the odds or suffering average products if they aren't up to scratch.

**At what age do you think 'screens' are okay?** Difficult question. I don't think screens per se are a problem. The issue is how they interact with them. I'd prefer to think that Ella's interaction with computers and TV will come naturally, when both she and us are ready for it. Until then, we don't force it but we allow her to look at pictures on the computer if she wants to. We allow as little TV as possible right now.

**How do you feel about commercial toys and branding? Are you first in the queue at midnight on Christmas Eve for this year's must-have toy?** All the more reason to not have your child drawn in by TV and internet advertising. There is nothing wrong with having a desire for a particular item; as a child I certainly recall being in this position. But I also recall not getting things I wanted and to be honest, it wasn't that bad.

**Your top three tips for imperfectly natural parenting?** Make sure you're educated about the options (I rely on Lynne for this mainly). Don't measure your views against others. Just do what you feel is right and trust your instincts (or your wife's!). If you need support, go on the internet and find like-minded virtual communities. See the results for yourself in the quality of your own life and the development of your child.

**Parenting pleasures – what do you most love about being a dad? What are your imperfections?** Seeing the world all over again through a child's eyes and re-igniting that sense of wonder. Watching them develop. Feeling part of a family.

**Anything else you'd like to share to help towards an imperfectly natural world?** Research the options, do what you believe is right for you and don't look for justification in others. You probably won't get it. Question the herd mentality.

# Family lifestyles

'Pretty much all the honest truth telling in the world is done by children.'
OLIVER WENDELL HOLMES

# Attachment parenting

What is attachment parenting? It sounds new and trendy but it's actually very old-fashioned. It's about many of the subjects I cover in this book, including breastfeeding, baby-wearing, safe co-sleeping and positive discipline. It's about being attached – avoiding long periods of separation between parent and child. Perhaps we should just call it conscious parenting, because it's also about letting go and allowing your child to grow.

## Letting go

Somewhere along the way, progress has brought with it an industry around bringing up children. As good parents, we are expected to buy toys and gadgets and a wide range of entertainment from baby French classes to fun tumbling sessions. There is a temptation to overcomplicate and fill up our days with a whole range of activities for our tiny babies and toddlers when, actually, we should be simply getting on with the business of living.

Jean Liedloff in The Continuum Concept (Penguin) says: 'It would help immeasurably if we could see babycare as a non-activity. We should learn to regard it as nothing to do. Working, shopping, cooking, cleaning, walking and talking with friends are things to do, to make time for, to think of as activities. The baby (with other children) is simply brought along as a matter of course. No special time need be set aside for him apart from the minutes devoted to changing his nappies. His bath can be part of his mother's. Breastfeeding need not stop all other activity either. It's only a matter of changing one's baby-centred thought patterns to those more suitable for a capable, intelligent being whose nature it is to enjoy work and the companionship of other adults.'

Apart from the wonderful few weeks of babymoon when you really are in recovery and bonding mode, life should go on as normal and the baby should just fit in. If they're treated with respect as little human beings, they will respond beautifully to watching and 'helping' as you go about your daily work. You don't need all the plans, arrangements, paraphernalia and worries that can come with trying to choreograph your life. Just give your baby his own space, let him discover, amuse and create in his own new world. Remember,

simple is good, and let him become a part of his new family, interacting in a natural way. Be a relaxed parent!

# Positive discipline

'Not only is example the best way to teach, it is the only way.'

ALBERT SCHWEITZER, MD

Things just aren't quite the same as they were when we were kids. We, for the most part, were told what to do and we didn't usually question it. These days, children re different, although cynics might say that children are much the same and it is society that has changed as we have become unable to discipline our children. I believe children really are different. They seem to come into the world much more 'knowing' and they demand our respect. Often they ask incredibly intelligent questions, even at a very young age and they will question our commands. To answer 'because I said so' isn't always enough.

As a parent, you want to offer unconditional love, yet you know that boundaries are important, which means putting some consistent measures in place. Don't set out with the idea that children are intrinsically naughty, that if you give them something they ask for, they are being spoilt and that they are wilful, manipulative and need to be suppressed.

The 'children should be seen and not heard' brigade are, thankfully, long gone but our education system is still such that it relies on orders being issued and children behaving as they're told, without question. Just sometimes, though, these bright kids will have thought of a better way while we're all still entrenched in old nineteenth-century ideas. Consider the fact that the word 'discipline' comes from the word 'disciple', which means 'to follow in the footsteps of'. As a parent, are you leading by example?

Most parents will agree that spanking a child doesn't really work. If you smack your child, you are probably doing it for one reason only – because you are the one who's lost control. You will be amazed at how furious this little love of your life can make you, but smacking your toddler because he keeps sitting on the baby won't make him stop. Children who are smacked learn to do what's right, not by connecting with their innate ability to choose right from wrong, but through fear of pain. It teaches them merely to find ways of avoiding the pain, the obvious one being to commit the crime out of sight. Children have a natural instinct for doing what's best for themselves and, if you leave them alone, odds are they'll make the right choices. Even the occasional wrong choice can be a valuable lesson in cause and effect, within reason of course. They don't need to learn a valuable lesson by running in front of a bus. Positive discipline, rather than removing free choice, is about empowering your children to accept and understand the guidelines in life and choose wisely when confronted with all the good and evil the big world has to offer.

A great read on relaxed parenting is Do Not Disturb - The Benefits of Relaxed Parenting for You and Your Child by Deborah Jackson. Another excellent book is How to Talk So Kids Will Listen and Listen So Kids Will Talk by Adele Faber and Elaine Mazlish.

## Enjoy your children

'Perhaps the greatest social service that can be rendered by anybody to the country and to mankind is to bring up a family.'
GEORGE BERNARD SHAW

Children can be annoying, frustrating, unpredictable, uncompromising and totally exhausting, but boring they are not. Children live in the here and now and they are incredibly inventive and enthusiastic. If plonked in front of a TV screen while you get on with your business for hours on end, they will become dullards and probably get cabin fever and play up. When you connect with a child, even, dare I say it, 'find' your child, it can all change in an instant. So, make time for them because one-on-one is all they want from you. A game of peepo is worth a million toys and they would (if

they could) happily trade them for half an hour of your time. They also thrive on the continual interaction recommended in 'Letting go' (see page 195). Include them in your group and family conversations. Even at two, they understand more than you think!

## Sharing and support

This is an important part of attachment parenting because there are so many like-minded people who want to share ideas. If what you need is a listening ear and help with parenting issues, mums and dads are actually pretty good at supporting each other. There are burgeoning online communities where you can even sort out your pressing issues at 2 a.m? If you want to, you can remain anonymous and, whatever you're going through, it's likely that someone else will have experienced it too. One of my favourite forums is **www.ukparents.co.uk**, and **www.mums net.co.uk** is another great one. There's also support and lots of information at **www.babygroe.co.uk**.

Much smaller (but perfectly formed!) is my own forum at **www.imperfectly natural.com** and the inspirational membership group **www.groups.yahoo. com/group/imperfectly_natural_parents _uk**. Another excellent community resource to check out is **www.develop yourchild**.co.uk.

## Professional support

'When we have children we are either woken to our own childhood pain and work on healing it or we inflict it on our children'

JACQUELINE A. WOOD.

Some parents have benefited greatly from going down this route and there are many organisations willing to help. Life coaches who specialise in parenting skills (**www.parentingpeople.co.uk**) can help with personal issues centring on defining goals for yourself and your family, and you'll usually find if you change your behaviour, the child does too! Some local initiatives run free parenting courses, so ask around. Try **www.surestart.gov.uk**. Many of these individuals and companies offer counselling sessions over the phone.

## Single parents

Firstly, whether you're a single parent through choice or a break-up, it's not somewhere I've been, so I'm not the one to be giving you advice. However, I have many friends who are single parents and, I have to tell you, I am so impressed by their resolve, their determination and, in every case, their absolute commitment to their children. Many women find a strength and resourcefulness that makes it work for them, sometimes against the odds.

This is the story of one imperfectly natural single parent, Sarah Barnard (of **www.ethicstrading.com**, see pages 26–7). 'I was in a relationship for sixteen years and had two children during that time. Then it ended. There were many reasons and I'd rather not go into them here but, in 2005, I asked my partner to leave. We shared a council house and agreed that it was best for the children to stay there. They were five and two at the time.

'While working through the disintegration of the relationship, I struggled with the kids. My son (the older one) became angry and aggressive; my younger daughter became clingy and wouldn't leave my side. I found my greatest support was an online community. I have some local friends who proved wonderful but the ones online got me through the dark times when I didn't want to go to bed. I was often up till the wee small hours in a state of "Oh hell, what have I done? How on earth am I going to cope?"

'But I did cope, I am coping. I had children to care for. I had a business to run. Both the children and the business suffered while I pulled my head out of the fog but I did pull it out. I am more than coping now, I am thriving. Now the children are so much happier and the business is booming.

'Through it all and, even now, I value most the support I've had from friends. I found telling them what was happening was liberating and talking through various options helped clear my mind. I discovered a couple of wonderful websites with single-parent forums and received a lot of support from my local Surestart.' Visit the Single Parents Advice Network (**www.spa-network.com**).

Hats off to you, Sarah! (Great soapnuts, by the way!) See pages 168–73 for more information on starting your own business and being a WAHM – working at home mum.

# Family fun

## Holidays

You'll have seen the ads on your screen at Christmas time promising a holiday of a lifetime in the sun – adults only. You've probably also heard of child hotels where, for an astronomical price, you can leave your beloved children in the care of well-trained nannies while you go away. By now, I think you'll know that my stance on that one would turn the air blue. You'll have many friends I'm sure who go on expensive foreign holidays with the kids, check them into a kids' club all week and never see them, but if you want to build family relationships and have fun with your kids, you need to have some holidays together and spend time enjoying each other's company. Chances are, though, they'll be nothing like the holidays you enjoyed 'BC'.

When we had our first child, we realised fairly quickly that jetting off to New York for quick shopping trips would be a thing of the past. Little did we realise just how difficult it would be to find a break that could provide anything in the way of relaxation with a baby in tow.

Later, with another few children joining the fold, we were pretty shocked to find that in the UK there is still an assumption that, if you have children, you want to go to a holiday camp or a theme park if you've got any cash at all or, if not, you'll manage in a scruffy campsite. Wrong! Some of us still want a little bit of pampering and luxury when we go away. We want excellent food and wine, luxurious lounges with open fires in winter and terraces in summer and we want our children to be welcomed with open arms. We want healthy food for them to eat at a suitable time, a choice of entertainment and really high-quality childcare or kids' clubs that they rejoice in going to, rather than a poorly stocked playroom with a surly-looking work-experience nanny watching over them.

First, going abroad. It's scary negotiating airports, baggage, toddlers on flights and, if you have more than a few children, the constant worry that you might have forgotten one somewhere. With one child, it's a delight. I loved visiting Spain with our one-year-old and would recommend it to any couple with a new baby as a time to

bond in a country full of friendly, chilled people. Anyone who has been to Europe will know how it welcomes children. It's quite normal for families in Spain and Italy to be dining out late at night with the waiter entertaining the toddler and a stranger at the next table rocking the baby. Here in Britain, we just don't have the same attitude to kids but, fortunately, it's changing, as UK breaks become more popular. There are now a few very good family-friendly hotels and restaurants which really welcome young children and you aren't treated like lepers as a family. Look at the excellent travel site **www.babygoes2.com**.

For crashing waves, sandy beaches and top-notch child friendliness, I love the Bedruthan Steps Hotel on the North Cornish Coast (**www.bedruthan stepshotel.co.uk**), winners of the Sustainable Tourism Champion 2005 award. It's also quite near to the Eden Project, a great eco-friendly awareness experience for children. For other family friendly hotels, see **www.luxuryfamily hotels.co.uk**.

If you've always fancied a timeshare arrangement but just can't face jetting abroad with young kids and paraphernalia, check out a new timeshare project, again in my beloved Cornwall. Trelowarren Estate (**www.trelowarren.com**) offers what it calls Eco-timeshare, where you buy a regular holiday in a green building at

today's prices. For some great ideas for eco-friendly global holidays, from a tipi holiday through to a week on an organic farm, check out **www.little-earth.co.uk**. There are also all kinds of foreign holidays and adventure holidays that promote sustainability available at **www.responsibletravel.com**.

## Greetings campers!

Trust me, they may only be toddlers now but if you've got boys, you will have to camp. Until recently, I simply could not see the attraction of travelling miles across the country with your house on your back in order to arrive at a soggy field with no electricity or running water but, as with so many things, I've exercised my right to change my mind and it seems I'm not the only one. Twelve million people in Britain now choose camping as their annual holiday

# Imperfectly natural parent

**Your name, age, your children**
Maggie Howell, 38, three boys –
Joseph 5, Toby 3 and Jacob 18
months.

**Occupation?** Marketing and sales
manager. Now – natal hypnotherapist
and Doula **www.natalhypnotherapy.
co.uk**

**Birth experiences – natural/assisted?** All three of
the boys were born naturally at home with no other
pain relief than self-hypnosis. I LOVE giving birth – my
challenge is going to be stopping myself from getting
pregnant again and again!!!

**Did the baby's birth impact in any way on the
first few weeks – positively or negatively?** My first
and subsequent births were so awesome and so
empowering that I have since carved out a completely
new career, lifestyle and business for me and my family
based on helping other women to have a better birth
experience.

**How was breastfeeding?** I loved breastfeeding and
had no problems at all after the initial sore nipples.

**Your emotional state for the first six months?**
After six months I had decided to retrain as a clinical
hypnotherapist to learn more about what I had
experienced during birth. It was like I had found my
calling – being an earth mother! (Despite my very
corporate, capitalist approach to life before having
children.)

**Your physical health?** After having Jacob, I did have
a vaginal prolapse which was not very pleasant. Since
Jacob was about a year old, I have not really had any
problems with the prolapse.

**When did your figure return? Did you exercise?**
Because of the breastfeeding, I got my figure back

really quickly. With my first baby, it was about three
months before I was back to my pre-pregnancy
weight – I actually weighed less than before I was
pregnant! Marvellous!

**How was your relationship with your partner?**
With our first son, we had both agreed that we
wanted to follow attachment parenting and he was
very supportive of our choice to co-sleep and long-
term breastfeed.

**Nappies – if cloth, which type do your prefer
and why?** We have pretty much tried all the options.
With all three boys, we have used elimination
communication (relying on the natural cues a baby
gives when it needs to eliminate). Before then we
had used a variety of different cotton nappies,
including Motherease, and straight-forward cotton
squares. With the other two, I used a combination
of cloth and disposables.

**Over the age of one, what do your children eat
frequently?** Exactly what we eat. We have always
eaten together as a family

**Junk food/sweets?** They tend to get sweets from
others i.e. grandparents, aunts etc. so we only buy
biscuits, good-quality chocolate and ice-creams, which
we all love.

**How is their general health?** Excellent – none of
them have been vaccinated and they are all long-term
breastfed. They hardly get any of the colds and
infections going around, though Toby did get meningo-
encephalitis a year ago, which was awful – he was in
intensive care for two days and in hospital for a week.

**What's in your medicine cupboard for the kids?**
Homeopathy kit, acupressure bands, eucalyptus oil,
other essential oils, tiger balm, bob the builder
plasters, buttercup cough syrup and an emergency
bottle of Calpol – due to go out of date soon!

**What do you do to keep 'sane' what do you do for 'me' time?** Not much!! I LOVE train journeys when I can buy a gossipy magazine, a large chai latte and just indulge myself with no one asking anything of me.

**Sex (or lack of)?** Ummm!! When we have the energy, we have a great sex life – it is just not that often any more. I think it has been really hard for my husband as he would like more but realises that at this time in our lives there are other priorities and other pleasures.

**Skincare – soaps, moisturizers, sunscreen** In spite of years of encouragement from my mum to cleanse, tone, moisturise, I have one pot of Nivea that I use after a shower.

**How do you deal with challenging behaviour?** I notice that things all go pear-shaped when I am stressed, otherwise everything runs pretty smoothly – lesson learnt there! I try to use positive language/behaviour and follow the principle 'Talk to kids so they listen and listen to kids so they talk'.

**What do you hear yourself saying to your children often that you wish you didn't?** The word 'naughty' (it is such a useless word that does not teach a child anything about how to do things better).

**Do you employ childcare?** Yes, we now have a nanny four days a week who is brilliant. I so don't like the word nanny as it conjures up all sorts of images – she is simply Becka, who loves the kids and they love her.

**As a family, how green are you 10 is dark and leafy, 1 is a faint hint of peppermint.** About a 7 – recycling most things, cloth nappies, long-lasting light bulbs, growing our own vegetables etc. I'd love to have our own windmill, solar panels, eco-friendly car, small-holding etc.

**Do you consider fair-trade/ethical trading?** Yes, a bit, but not as much as we could, we shop a lot at Lidl so let the side down a bit there!

**What's your top ten eco-family tip?** Recycle, avoid disposable nappies, do not use all the ridiculous zillions of chemical cleaner products, babies do not need any soap, shampoo, lotions and potions, do not over-vaccinate (if at all), grow your own vegetables.

**How do you feel about commercial toys and branding? Are you first in the queue at midnight on Christmas Eve for this year's must-have toy?** We have managed to avoid them so far! For presents, we have asked all relatives not to buy them loads of stuff but instead to spend time with them and take them out on special days.

**Your top three tips for imperfectly natural parenting?** There is no such thing as a perfect mother. If you are happy, your kids are happy. Get as much help from friends and family as possible – we were designed to live in communities, not in individual box units.

**Parenting pleasures – what do you most love about being a mum?** Waking up with three soft, cuddly, beautiful children all around me…seeing their confidence grow, watching them interact with strangers…hearing them call my name to show me something amazing that they have just discovered …getting love notes from the boys left in my briefcase…not worrying about what other people think about the way I parent…and more…and more…

**What are your imperfections?** Hiding chocolate for myself, enjoying time away from the boys, wishing our nanny could stay on another hour so I can relax after work.

**Anything else you'd like to share to help towards an imperfectly natural world?** You don't need the majority of things that are in the shops or magazines. There is no need to compare your children to others – every one is an individual, everyone has a different learning style a different coping strategy.

and loads more take short breaks. After one week, I looked like a shipwreck survivor but we all adored it! It seems that camping is cool, so consider yourself warned!

I also have friends who tell me that another seemingly untrendy idea that has become cool again is youth hostelling (**www.yha.org.uk**). A youth hostel can be an excellent, good-value base at which to have a few days away with the kids, and lots of the bigger hostels offer family rooms and facilities (and no, you don't have to do the washing up!).

## Days out

It's amazing fun just to stroll through the park with toddlers in all weathers, such is their wonder at inspecting the smallest twig or soggy leaf. If you want to head off on a day trip, you won't have a better time or discover more about the environment than at the Centre for Alternative Technology in Wales (**www.cat.org.uk**).You can also volunteer to work there for a while and stay in one of their eco-cabins.

In Hertfordshire there is a wonderfully reconstructed Iron Age farmstead (or encampment) – Celtic Harmony (**www. celticharmony.org**). We were asked to bring a totally compostable after-use packed lunch, which got me thinking – until we came up with the idea of huge lettuce leaves tied around sandwiches! The kids had their faces daubed, made some incredible clay pendants and played Iron Age musical instruments.

There are also a host of educational and green activities awaiting the whole family at The Magdalen project, an organic farm and education centre in Dorset (**www.the magdalenproject.org.uk**). For specifically sustainable activities, subscribe to the Green Parent magazine (**www.thegreen parent.co.uk**) and have a look at **www.naturalmatters.net**.

City breaks are fantastic for kids and it's not just London that offers excellence in museums and tourism. There are lots of ideas for holidays, activities, camps and more at **www.eparenting.co.uk**.

## Gardening

You probably realise I'm a big fan of kids being outdoors in almost all weathers. Children need fresh air for long stretches at a time and gardening is a fantastic way of getting exercise too. It also attunes them with nature, helps them think creatively and appreciate the environment and there's a wealth of educational opportunities involved, ranging from biology and science to geography and ecology. Of course, with children it has to be relatively instant so you will need a low maintenance area for the kids to claim as their patch. Herbs are fantastic and can be grown in pots on windowsills if you don't have a garden. If you want inspiration, The National Trust

(www.national trust.org.uk) runs family gardening days at many of their homes and gardens.

It's hard to beat the Kitchen Garden project in West London (www.kitchen garden.org.uk). Their regular open days attract thousands of visitors and, along with complete tours of the gardens, you can pick the herbs and even take some home with instructions as to how to bake herby bread. There's a working beehive and you can offer, as a family, to drop in and do the gardening. There's also the excellent Plant for Life initiative (www.plantfor life.info), which aims to encourage children to interact with nature and get their hands dirty.

If all you're cultivating right now is couch potatoes and you're still not convinced, I highly recommend reading Saving Our Children from Nature-Deficit Disorder by Richard Louv (Algonquin Books of Chapel Hill).

## Family fitness

When it comes to sports and fitness, I'm afraid it's not my bag. However, as my opinion on camping had to change, so did my views on joining a gym. After some coercion from friends, I tried the Next Generation Club (www.nextgeneration clubs.co.uk), a gym with the primary aim of creating a family environment. We went to look around and suddenly

I saw my family's leisure, fitness and playtime all rolled into one. They have a complete programme for kids and another for babies and toddlers. There's a crèche, a kids' gym with child-sized fitness equipment, even a mini activity world for toddlers. We love the baby yoga, and the café offers children's buffets twice a week, which is great for their social life. There's an open-air pool as well as the indoor one with spa (divine if the weather is good) and, wait for it, I've discovered the joys of playing tennis. We now play tennis as a family and have a huge laugh. There are fifteen or so around the country and if you don't live near one, just check that the gym you're considering joining is also big on families.

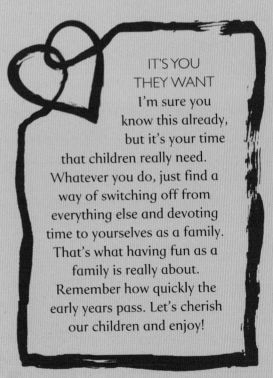

IT'S YOU
THEY WANT
I'm sure you
know this already,
but it's your time
that children really need.
Whatever you do, just find a
way of switching off from
everything else and devoting
time to yourselves as a family.
That's what having fun as a
family is really about.
Remember how quickly the
early years pass. Let's cherish
our children and enjoy!

# Recommended reading

Throughout this book I refer to a bunch of people who have inspired me and helped guide my parenting choices. These are their books and they all come highly recommended!

**The Continuum Concept by Jean Liedloff** (Arkana) I dread to think how my life would have been had I not read **The Continuum Concept**. I wish I'd read it during pregnancy as it would have saved me those early weeks of wondering if it really was okay to follow my intuition when it told me to sleep with my baby, feed him whenever he seemed to want it and keep him close to me in a sling most of the time.

**Three in a Bed, and Do Not Disturb by Deborah Jackson** (Bloomsbury) Deborah Jackson was the next author I was thrilled to come across. Her more Westernised approach to the ideals of attachment parenting has made me a huge fan.

**Primal Health by Dr Michel Odent** (Clairview Books) A more inspirational man you could never wish to meet. A pioneering birth guru, he's written lots of other great books too.

**The Gentle Birth Method by Dr Gowri Motha and Dr Karen Swan Macleod** (Harper Collins) Dr Motha has become quite famous as the birth guru to the stars but I was lucky enough to find her before her meteoric rise to fame. She is, without question, the woman I am most grateful to (apart, perhaps, from my own mother) for everything she has shared with me and for her encouragement, support and incredible physical energy through my four pregnancies and subsequent natural births with almost instant recovery (**www.gentlebirthmethod. com**).

**The No-Cry Sleep Solution by Elizabeth Pantley** (Contemporary Books) I was told of the wonderful no-cry sleep solution at a time when I desperately needed it. For all my holistic living and natural nurturing, I can be honest and tell you I came close to trying the 'cry it out' method myself. Thank you, Elizabeth Pantley, for helping me to wind down to sleep like a baby again. Not overnight, but over time, this rational, gentle book helped me realise that I was not alone in the quest for sleep and that there were gentle methods on offer to solve the problem.

**Birth and Beyond, The Definitive Guide to Your Pregnancy, Your Birth, Your Family by Yehudi Gordon** (Vermilion) Yehudi Gordon was the obstetrician overseeing all of my births. He was another totally inspirational birth guru and one of the pioneers for active birth and water birth in the UK, who fully understands the needs of pregnant women and treats us like intelligent individuals. **Birth and Beyond** is his most recent book.

**What Really Works for Kids – the Insiders Guide to Natural Health for Mums and Dads** by Susan Clark (Bantam Press) Susan is a health journalist and author of a couple of books without which I could not have existed. **What Really Works for Kids** is a fantastically comprehensive, no-nonsense book about food additives and alternatives to allopathic medicine for common ailments. She's a mother herself and is brave enough to tell you exactly what is in the average fish finger, so be warned!

**Cleaning Yourself to Death: How Safe is Your Home?** and **Living Dangerously: Are Everyday Toxins Making You Sick?** by Pat Thomas (Newleaf) Pat Thomas is author of several books on environmental and health issues and writes a lot for **The Ecologist**. She pulls no punches and has written some excellent books.

I also recommend these books:

**How to Survive the Terrible Twos** by Caroline Dunford (White Ladder Press)

**Liberated Parents Liberated Children** by Adele Faber, Elaine Mazlish (Piccadilly Press)

**How to Talk So Kids Will Listen and Listen So Kids Will Talk** by Adele Faber and Elaine Mazlish (Piccadilly Press)

**Siblings Without Rivalry** by Adele Faber and Elaine Mazlish (Piccadilly Press)

**The Secret of Happy Children** by Steve Biddulph (HarperCollins)

**Natural Baby: How to Optimise Your Child's Development in the First Year of Life** by Janet Balaskas and Anthea Sieveking (Gaia Books)

**The Indigo Children** by Lee Carroll and Jan Tober (Hay House)

**Little Angels** (aka **The Discipline Book**) by Bill and Martha Sears (Hodder & Stoughton), also **The Baby Book**

**What Parents Can Do With and For Their Children From Birth to Aged Six** by Rahima Baldwin Dancy (Celestial Arts)

**Understanding Your Crying Baby: Why Babies Cry, How Parents Feel and What You Can Do About It** by Sheila Kitzinger (Carroll & Brown Publishers)

**Dumbing Us Down: The Hidden Curriculum of Compulsory Schooling** by John Taylor Gatto (New Society Books, Philadelphia, USA)

# Directory

**Forum**
www.imperfectlynatural.co.uk

## From newborn to toddler

### RECOVERY AFTER BIRTH
**Organic sanitary protection**
www.natracare.co.uk

**National Childbirth Trust**
www.nct.org.uk

**Bowen Technique**
www.thebowentechnique.com

**Birth preparation/Ayurvedic diets/teething pendants**
www.gentlebirthmethod.com

**Essential oils and blends**
www.tortuerouge.co.uk.

**Post-natal depression**
www.apni.org
www.mama.co.uk

### BREASTFEEDING
www.ukamb.org
**Breastfeeding after reduction**
www.bfar.org

www.babydayz.co.uk

**Breastfeeding counsellors and advice**
Association of Breastfeeding Mothers
www.abm.me.uk
La Leche League
www.laleche.org.uk
National Childbirth Trust
www.nctpregnancyandbabycare.com
Breastfeeding network
www.breastfeedingnetwork.org.uk

**Breastfeeding bras, pillows etc.**
www.avent.com
www.babydayz.co.uk
www.bravadodesigns.co.uk
www.breastfeeding.com
www.expressyourselfmums.co.uk
www.lactivist.co.uk
www.laitdamour.com
www.lasinoh.co.uk
www.maternityandnursing.co.uk
www.nctms.co.uk
www.spiritofnature.co.uk

**Formula-feeding**
www.buffalomilk.co.uk
www.goodnessdirect.co.uk
www.ulula.co.uk

### NAPPIES
**Information on cloth nappies**

www.crnp.org.uk
www.nappyalliance.com
www.realnappycampaign.com
www.teamlollipop.co.uk
www.thenappylady.com
www.wen.org.uk

## Cloth nappies
www.babyarmadillo.com
www.freerangekids.co.uk
www.twinkleontheweb.co.uk
www.underthegooseberrybush.co.uk

## Eco-disposables
www.greenbaby.co.uk
www.spiritofnature.co.uk

## Laundry
www.colourcatcher.co.uk

## Soapnuts
www.ethicstrading.com

## Laundry balls
www.aquaball.com

## GREEN CLEAN
www.aquaball.com
www.babyscents.co.uk
www.homescents.co.uk
www.naturalclean.co.uk
www.natural-house.co.uk

## BABY SKIN
## Baby bathtime
www.tummytub.co.uk

## Organic towels
www.organictowel.co.uk

## Organic linen
www.peopletree.co.uk

## Nursery cleaner
www.babyscents.co.uk

## Baby skincare
www.coconoil.com
www.earth-friendly-baby.co.uk
www.greenpeople.co.uk
www.junglesale.com
www.lavera.co.uk
www.naturalchild.co.uk
www.purepotions.co.uk
www.sensitiveskincareco.com
www.spiritofnature.co.uk
www.thenaturalcollection.com

## Suncare
www.oliveorganic.co.uk
www.suntogs.co.uk

## Essential oils and aromatherapy products
www.eoco.org.uk
www.essentiallyoils.com
www.wristangel.co.uk

## TEETH
www.bickiepegs.co.uk
www.greenpeople.co.uk
www.lavera.co.uk
www.mionegroup.com
www.naturaltoothbrush.com

## BABY CLOTHING AND BAGS

www.cut4cloth.co.uk
www.eco-eco.co.uk
www.greenbaby.co.uk
www.star-child.co.uk
www.tattybumpkin.com

### Eco-friendly bags

www.earthpak.com
www.turtlebags.co.uk

## FAIR-TRADE CLOTHING

www.labourbehindthelabel.org

## BABY-WEARING AND SWADDLING

www.babyarmadillo.co.uk
www.brightsparkslings.co.uk
www.kari-me.co.uk
www.littlepossums.co.uk
www.thecarryingkind.co.uk

### Forum and advice on slings

www.slingmeet.co.uk

## SLEEPING
### Relaxation tapes

www.relaxkids.com

### Bed linens and furniture

www.greenfibres.co.uk
www.handmadehammocks.co.uk
www.smilechild.co.uk
www.spiritofnature.co.uk
www.tuttibambini.co.uk

## BABY-PROOFING
### Alternatives to plastics

www.babybfree.com
www.babypots.com
www.greenbabyco.com
www.tipslimited.com

## BABY-SIGNING

www.babysigning.co.uk
www.happyhandz.co.uk
www.tinytalk.co.uk

## OUT OF NAPPIES

www.pottywhisperer.com

## TOYS AND PLAY

www.anara.co.uk
www.barefoot-books.com
www.greenfibres.com
www.huckaback.co.uk
www.myriadonline.co.uk
www.nigelsecostore.co.uk
www.ninnynoodlenoo.com
www.toygiant.co.uk
www.uk.freecycle.org

# Good food for mother and baby

## ORGANIC LOCAL PRODUCE

www.aboutorganics.co.uk
www.cooksdelight.co.uk
www.ethicalfoodcompany.co.uk
www.farma.org.uk
www.farmersmarkets.net
www.local-farmers-
    markets.co.uk/contact.html

www.rocketgardens.co.uk

## FOOD AND NUTRITION FOR HEALTHY CHILDREN
### Nutrition and qualified nutritionists
www.bant.org.uk
www.thefooddoctor.com

### Organic babyfood
www.bathorganicbabyfood.co.uk
www.goodnessdirect.co.uk
www.organix.com
www.ulula.co.uk

### Rainbow food charts
www.lemonburst.co.uk

### Funky bibs
www.snuglo.com

### FunPod
www.littlehelper.co.uk

## THE SUGAR RUSH
### Sweets and treats
www.glutenfreebakery.co.uk
www.lemonburst.co.uk
www.stores.ebay.co.uk/
    The-Organic-Sweet-Shop

### Sugar substitutes
www.groovyfood.co.uk
www.perfectsweet.co.uk
www.stevia.com

## SNACK TREATS
www.coconoil.com

www.ellaskitchen.co.uk
www.supajus.co.uk

## FOOD ALLERGIES
www.bant.org.uk
www.hk4health.co.uk
www.naet.co.uk
www.nutripeople.co.uk
www.en.wikipedia.org/wiki/Bioresonance_
    therapy

# Imperfectly naturally . . . unwell

### Homeopathy
www.a-r-h.org
www.helios.co.uk
www.homeopathy-soh.org

### Herbs and teas
www.hambledonherbs.com

### Medical herbalists
www.nimh.org.uk

### Vitamins, minerals and homeopathic remedies
www.ainsworths.com
www.biocare.co.uk
www.livingnature.co.uk
www.viridian-nutrition.com

## CUTS AND WOUNDS
### Manuka honey
www.naturesnectar.co.uk

## SKIN PROBLEMS

www.neemtree.info

www.sensitveskincareco.com

## SORE LIPS

www.naturallytejas.com

www.spieziaorganics.com

## SUNBURN

www.greenpeople.co.uk

www.oliveorganic.co.uk

www.sun-togs.co.uk

## HEAD LICE

www.lemonburst.co.uk

www.nits.net

## FLOWER ESSENCES

www.indigoessences.com

www.tortuerouge.co.uk

## TO VACCINATE OR NOT TO VACCINATE?

www.immunisation.nhs.uk

www.vaccination.org.uk

www.wddty.co.uk

# Looking After Yourself

## SKIN AND HAIR CARE

www.aubreyorganics.com

www.coconoil.com

www.essentialspirit.co.uk

www.eva-cosmetics.de

www.hempgarden.co.uk

www.nealsyardremedies.com,

www.oliveorganic.co.uk

www.purelyforyou.co.uk

www.sensitiveskincareco.com

www.summernaturals.co.uk

### Cosmetics

www.avea.co.uk

www.livingnature.co.uk

www.lilylolo.co.uk

www.sheerorganics.com

www.totallyorganics.co.uk

### Natural deodorants

www.crystaldeodorant.com

www.lemonburst.co.uk

www.naturalcollection.com

### Hair

www.herbatint.co.uk

www.sensitiveskincareco.com

### Nails

www.greenhands.co.uk

www.santecosmetics.co.uk

www.suncoateurope.com

### Mole screening

www.themoleclinic.com

### Himalayan salt

www.kudosrocksalt.co.uk

www.saltshack.co.uk

## FEMININE CARE

www.ladycarehealth.com

www.mooncup.co.uk

## KEEPING FIT
www.chi-machine.co.uk
www.integralnutrition.co.uk
www.juicemaster.com
www.integralnutrition.co.uk

## THERAPIES
www.fht.org.uk
www.wellbeingnetwork.co.uk

### Magnetic therapy
www.ecoflow.plc.uk

### Cranial osteopathy
www.cranial.org.uk

### Craniosacral therapy
www.ccst.co.uk

### Bowen Technique
www.thebowentechnique.com

### Light therapy
www.litebook.com
www.sad.uk.com
www.wholisticresearch.com

## SEX
www.pelvictoner.co.uk

## RETURNING TO WORK
### Information and advice
www.dti.gov.uk
www.motheratwork.co.uk

### Support and forums
www.mumszone.co.uk

www.nationalchildbirthtrust.co.uk
www.netmums.co.uk
www.ukparents.co.uk

### Working at home mums
www.DownshiftingWeek.com
www.mumzmall.co.uk
www.organisedmum.co.uk

## CHILDCARE
www.aupairworld.net
www.nannytax.co.uk

## GETTING WHAT YOU WANT FROM LIFE
www.wellbeingnetwork.com

### Parent coaching
www.parentingpeople.co.uk

### Feng shui
www.fengshui4you.co.uk

### Alternative education
www.naturekids.co.uk

## ANOTHER BABY?
### Trying to conceive
www.bant.org
www.foresight-preconception.org.uk
www.fpa.org.uk/guide/contracep/natural.htm
www.gentlebirthmethod.com
www.goddessmums.com
www.natalhypnotherapy.co.uk
www.pinkforagirl.com

### Beautiful bump photos
www.tinabolton.co.uk

### Forums and support
www.groups.yahoo.com/group/imperfectly_
    natural_parents_uk
www.imperfectlynaturalwoman.co.uk
www.mumsnet.co.uk
www.picklesworld.com
www.pregnancyforum.co.uk
www.surestart.gov.uk
www.ukparents.co.uk

### Better birth experiences
www.birthlight.com
www.gentlewater.co.uk
www.homebirth.org.uk
www.independentmidwives.org.uk
www.onemotheronemidwife.org.uk

# Family lifestyles

### FAMILY FUN
### Advice and information
www.babygoes2.com
www.eparenting.co.uk

www.little-earth.co.uk
www.naturalmatters.net
www.responsibletravel.com
www.thegreenparent.co.uk

### Recommended holidays/days out
www.bedruthanstepshotel.co.uk
www.cat.org.uk
www.celticharmony.org
www.luxuryfamilyhotels.co.uk
www.themagdalenproject.org.uk
www.trelowarren.com
www.yha.org.uk

### Gardening
www.kitchengarden.org.uk
www.nationaltrust.org.uk
www.plantforlife.info
www.rocketgardens.co.uk

### Family fitness
www.nextgenerationclubs.co.uk

# Contact us
### To contact Janey, please email
janey@imperfectlynatural.co.uk

# Acknowledgements

A huge thanks to Euan Thorneycroft at AM Heath, and Amanda, Lucie, Clare and all at Orion Books.

I can't write a book on 'natural' parenting without thanking my four fantastic children Sonny, Buddy, Rocky and Lulu for teaching me so much. Thanks for all the glorious, messy, joyous moments.

Thanks to Gowri Motha – birth guru and godmother to the boys who guided me through four inspirational natural births.

I must big up Steve Wright and Tim Smith on Radio 2, who, much to their amusement, often seem to end up talking to the nation about breastfeeding and cloth nappies!

Thanks to everyone who made my first book such a success and to all my 'virtual' friends and all on my forum at www.imperfectlynatural.com. You are wonderfully supportive and knowledgeable.

Lastly, thanks and so much love to my husband Simon, referred to in this book as DH (Darling Husband), who at times has had to put his own career on the back burner to support me in my eco-endeavours.

# Photo credits

Tina Bolton 2–3,10, 13, 15, 30, 83, 148, 156, 167, 180, 187, 191; Terry Carne 201, 202; Geoff Crawford 142; Steve Double 20, 33, 48, 49, 50, 64, 65, 68, 73, 101, 102, 103, 104, 117, 126, 132, 145, 150R, 154; David Brook all others.

Thanks to Rosi Flood for her styling work.

# Illustrations

Robyn Neild 35; 95, 109, 160. 164, 203; Lemonburst.co.uk 123, 150L.

# Index